All About Powerboats

ALL ABOUT

Powerboats

Understanding Design and Performance

ROGER MARSHALL

INTERNATIONAL MARINE / McGRAW-HILL

Camden, Maine • New York • Chicago • San Francisco • Lisbon • London • Madrid
Mexico City • Milan • New Delhi • San Juan • Seoul • Singapore • Sydney • Toronto

International Marine

A Division of The McGraw-Hill Companies

10 9 8 7 6 5 4
Copyright © 2002 Roger Marshall

Library of Congress Cataloging-in-Publication Data
Marshall, Roger.
  All about powerboats : understanding design and performance / Roger Marshall.
     p.   cm.
Includes index.
  ISBN 0-07-136204-5 (pbk. : alk. paper)
 1. Motorboats—Design and construction. 2. Motorboats—Speed. I. Title.
  VM341 .M367 2002
  623.8′231—dc21
2001008508

Questions regarding the content of this book should be addressed to
International Marine
P.O. Box 220
Camden, ME 04843
www.internationalmarine.com

Questions regarding the ordering of this book should be addressed to
The McGraw-Hill Companies
Customer Service Department
P.O. Box 547
Blacklick, OH 43004
Retail customers: 1-800-262-4729
Bookstores: 1-800-722-4726

This book is printed on 70# Citation by R. R. Donnelley
Design by dcdesign
Page layout by Deborah Evans
Production management by Janet Robbins
Edited by Jonathan Eaton, Dan Spurr, David C. Brown, and Alex Barnett

Photo credits for pages 8–9 (left to right): Wellcraft Marine, Correct Craft, Correct Craft, David J. Shuler (courtesy Nordhavn), Wellcraft Marine, Wellcraft Marine, Luhrs Corporation, Cigarette, Wellcraft Marine, Aquasport, The Catamaran Company
Title page illustration by Steven L. Davis
Other photographs and illustrations by the author unless otherwise noted

Contents

Acknowledgments   ix

Chapter 1.   FACTORS IN POWERBOAT DESIGN   1
Powerboat Speed 4
Other Design Factors 6
    Seaworthiness / Range / Comfort / Cost

Chapter 2.   THE LANGUAGE OF HULL SHAPES   13
Reading the Lines 13
    Profile View / Plan View / Sectional View
Features of Hull Design 19
    Chines / Deadrise / Freeboard / Flare / Keels and Bilge
    Keels / Running Strakes / Trim Angle and Trim Tabs

Chapter 3.   HULL SHAPES   26
Displacement Hulls 26
    Trawler Yachts / Skinny Boats / Catamarans
Planing Hulls 36
    High-Speed Deep-V Hulls / Stepped Hulls
Fishing Hull Shapes 40
    Saltwater Flats Boats / Bass Boats / Offshore Sport-
    fishing Boats
Semiplaning or Transitional Hull Shapes 43
    Bow / Midbody / Stern
Summary 45
Common Questions 45
    A Rounded Hull or Chined Hull: Which Is Best? / How
    Fast Will It Go? / How Many People Can I Get Aboard? /
    What Range Can I Expect?

Chapter 4.   TOOLS TO HELP EVALUATE BOATS   47
    Speed–Length Ratio / Displacement–Length Ratio /
    Length-to-Beam Ratio / Power-to-Weight Ratio / Cubic
    Number / Prismatic Coefficient

Chapter 5.   POWERBOAT STYLING   50
    Hull Styling 50
      Developing the Sheerline / Developing the Bow and Stern
    Adding the Superstructure 55
      Avoiding Clutter

Chapter 6.   UNDERSTANDING STABILITY   59
    Factors Affecting Transverse Stability 60
      Form Stability / Center of Gravity / Chines and Chine Flats
    Longitudinal Stability 64
    Tender and Stiff Boats 64
    Stability at Large Angles of Heel 64
    Effects of Flooding on Stability 66

Chapter 7.   SEAWORTHINESS   68
    The Skill of the Skipper and Crew 68
    A Seaworthy Hull 69
    Seaworthiness Belowdecks 69
    Engine Room 70
    Seaworthiness on Deck 70

Chapter 8.   COMFORT   72
    A Comfortable Hull Shape 72
    Onboard Location Counts 73
    Stabilizers 73
      Passive Stabilizers / Active Stabilizers / Paravanes /
      Dynamic Stabilization
    Comfort on Deck 75
      Easy and Safe to Go Forward / Easy-to-Climb Ladders and

Stairwells / Easy to Work in the Cockpit or to Enjoy the Fantail / Fewer Steps between Deck Levels

Lighting for Comfort   77
Deck Lighting / Lighting in the Engine Room

Interior Comfort   79
Doors, Passageways, and Walkways / Bridge Layout / Sleeping Quarters / Bunk Dimensions / Bathrooms and Toilets

Designing for Good Maintenance   83

Storage   84
Electronics Storage / Galley Storage / Lockers / Refrigerator / Under the Cabin Sole / Overhead Storage / Engine Room Storage / Anchor Storage

Chapter 9.   POWERING YOUR BOAT   87
Early Engines   87

Basic Engine Types   88
Two-Stroke Cycle or "Two-Cycle" Engines (Gasoline) / Four-Stroke Cycle or "Four-Cycle" Engines (Gasoline) / Diesel Engines (Inboards)

Outboard Engines   91
Recent Outboard Engine Developments / Choosing an Outboard

Inboard Engines   97
The Latest Gasoline Inboard Engines / Diesel Inboard Engines / Gas or Diesel Inboard: Which One Is for You? / Single or Twin Engines?

Sterndrive Engines   101

Inboard, Outboard, or Sterndrive?   102

Jet Drive   103

Drive Train Components   103
Transmission / Propeller Shaft / Shaft Logs

Chapter 10.   PROPELLERS   105
Propeller Terminology   105

Increasing Your Propeller's Efficiency   109

Common Engine Solutions   111
Vibration / Noise

Chapter 11.   STEERING SYSTEMS   115
 Wheel Steering   115
  Hydraulic / Cable / Wire
 Other Types of Steering Systems   119
  Steering with a Whipstaff / Tiller Steering / Rack-and-Pinion
  Steering
 Rudders   121
 Steering with Twin Engines   122
  Backing Down

Chapter 12.   HOW A BOAT IS BUILT   123
 The Mold   123
  Making the Plug / Making the Mold
 Laying Up a Hull   124
  The Laminate / Interior Moldings / Vacuum-Assisted Resin
  Transfer Molding (VARTM)
 Evolution of Hull Materials   133
 Core Materials   133
 Resins   134
 Putting the Hull Together   136
  Production Boat Construction / Custom Boat Construction /
  Semicustom Boats / Safety

Appendix.   INFLATABLES   139
 Puncture Resistance   140
 Rigid-Bottom versus Soft-Bottom   141
 What to Look For: Features and Construction   142

Index   143

Acknowledgments

W H E N   Y O U   W R I T E a book, you often find that your knowledge and experiences of a particular subject are limited. Exactly this happened when I wrote this book. I asked my good friend Dean Clarke, executive editor of *Sport Fishing* magazine, to read the manuscript. Dean added many comments and suggestions that enhanced the manuscript greatly. So not only do you get the wisdom that I have accumulated, you also get the benefit of other highly experienced boaters when you buy this book. Thanks, Dean.

Another editor who read the rough manuscript was John Wooldridge, managing editor of *Motor Boating and Sailing* magazine. John added even more information based on his experiences both having fun in boats and reviewing them for the magazine.

A third editor who read the manuscript was Bill Sisson. The editor of *Soundings*, Bill has edited my column for that magazine for over five years. Needless to say, by now I trust his judgment. Bill and the able staff at *Soundings* comment on every column and almost always improve it in some small way. To their editing I owe several first and second place awards in the annual Boating Writers International marine journalism contest. Many of those same columns have been adapted for this book with the improvements made by the *Soundings* staff.

But I didn't seek comments only of editors. I asked Karl Seelig, a recreational boater, if I had missed anything that he wanted to know. Karl came up with several suggestions that also improved the overall content.

In addition, many manufacturers offered help. If I had engine questions, I generally referred them to Tony Esposito of Mercury Marine, who knew the right person to talk to if he didn't know the answer. Randy Hale III, of Hale Propeller, helped explain some of the intricacies of propeller tuning and the latest MRI measuring machine. Barry Carroll, of Carroll Marine in Bristol, Rhode Island, has been helpful on many occasions, as was Rich Worstell of Valiant Yachts. Gordon Hauser, of Wellcraft, answered questions or directed me to someone within his organization who could. Without the help of Jon Eaton, editor extraordinaire of International Marine, this book would not be what it is. Of course, there are many others who—often unwittingly—added experience and examples to the manuscript. To these people I owe my thanks.

Roger Marshall
Jamestown, Rhode Island

1

FACTORS IN POWERBOAT DESIGN

WHAT IS THE BEST hull shape for a powerboat? The answer, of course, is that there is no single, all-purpose "best." The most you can hope for is to identify an appropriate hull for the kind of boating you want to do. As you weigh the factors and attempt to balance speed with seaworthiness, comfort with fuel economy, and all of these with cost, you may decry the complexities, but remember to be thankful for them, too. Boating would be a lot less interesting if all boats looked alike.

If you want only to skim across flat water, shattering the early-morning calm, a light, flat-bottomed hull or a hydroplane will suit your purpose. The world speed record is currently owned by a jet-propelled hydroplane-style hull that ran at more than 317 miles per hour (about 500 kilometers per hour). With jet propulsion it had no propeller drag, and its bottom was about as flat longitudinally as a kitchen door. There are currently several attempts under way to break that record in similar boats, boats that sacrifice everything else in the single-minded pursuit of speed. It is predicted that some sort of hydroplane will break the sound barrier by the year 2010. These boats would shake your teeth out in a light chop and might come to grief on a single wave. For regular flat-water inshore races, three-point hydroplanes, such as *Miss Budweiser*, exceed 200 mph (322 kph). Or if drag boat racing is your choice, you can

The big, powerful *Miss Budweiser* can exceed 200 mph but needs flat water to do it in.

Miss Budweiser's tiny but powerful turbine engine: an unusual power plant for an unusual boat.

expect to accelerate to around 240 mph (386 kph) in five seconds from a standing start. Most of us, however, will be happier with a more practical hull form that can do a variety of things.

If you want to run at high speeds in a seaway, a deep-V hull is a much preferable shape. It won't go as fast as a hydroplane over smooth water, but it can attain speeds in excess of 100 mph (160 kph) and will slice through waves that would destroy the flat-bottomed boat. It will be strongly built, but at that speed the ride will still be uncomfortable. If you want it to make a challenging ocean passage without sacrificing speed, the boat will have to be much bigger, and in the future it might even morph into something like the Wave Piercer shown in the accompanying sketch.

If you want to fish offshore, a beamy, stable, moderate-displacement hull with a little V in the bottom may be best, keeping

This deep-V, planing design is used in a high-performance school in Florida run by Wellcraft Marine and can attain speeds up to 80 mph (129 kph). *(Wellcraft Marine)*

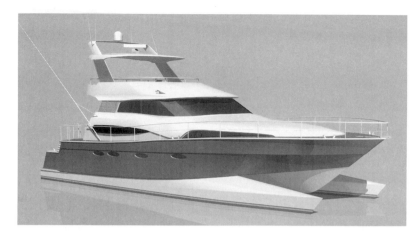

A 20-meter (66 ft.) Wave Piercer hull from New Zealand shows a new approach to going fast in high seas. The two forward hull projections pierce waves so that the boat does not pitch in a seaway, also extending its waterline length. (Craig Loomis Design Group Ltd.)

you relatively comfortable at trolling speeds when a deep-V hull would be rolling unmercifully.

For long-distance cruising, a heavy, relatively narrow, slightly V'd or round-bilge hull will get you there slowly (at 8–15 knots) but comfortably, with good fuel economy and good seakeeping ability.

In general, the faster you go, the more limited your range (the distance you can go on a full tank of fuel), and the rougher your journey. The trade-offs among speed, range, and comfort are inescapable, and the various approaches to reconciling these factors make the world of powerboat design fascinating. Hull designs and propulsion packages continue to evolve. The current speed record for electric boats is more than 70 mph (113 kph) from a boat that develops less than 125 hp. The current outboard-powered record stands at more than 175 mph (282 kph). And power catamarans offer new and interesting combinations of speed, stability, fuel economy, and comfort.

Some people use seaworthiness as a

The Luhrs 400 Open shows low freeboard aft for fishing, and much higher freeboard forward to keep seas off the deck and provide reserve buoyancy in large waves. (Luhrs Corp.)

A Nordhavn trawler yacht offers comfort and seakindliness at displacement speeds. *(David J. Shuler, courtesy Nordhavn)*

defining parameter for powerboats, while others think first of speed or range. Designers tend to consider speed and seaworthiness foremost, asking first what speed is needed and where the boat will operate. From these considerations flows everything else.

POWERBOAT SPEED

The factors that limit powerboat speed are cost, comfort of ride, carrying capacity, weight, range, and seaworthiness. An ultrafast boat will be expensive to build, lightly constructed, limited in the number of crew it can carry, limited in its seaworthiness, and subject to motions that can literally break a crew's back. Above all, speed costs money, which is why freight-carrying ships are slow for their length.

In the accompanying graph of boat speed versus propulsive power, there are three distinct operating regimes for a boat: displacement, semidisplacement (also known as *semiplaning* or *transitional*), and planing. Most displacement hulls are incapable of speeds much higher than 1.5 times the square root of waterline length, even with a very large engine. If the waterline length (LWL) is 36 feet (11 m), 9 knots is about as fast as a displacement boat will typically go. A semidisplacement boat is shaped and powered to go somewhat faster—say up to 15 knots or so on a 36-foot waterline—but although it bends the rules of hydrodynamic resistance, it cannot escape them. To do that you need a true planing hull, which uses hydrodynamic lift to rise up out of the water and reduce resistance. Planing boats may attain speeds of 7 to 10 times the square root of their waterline length.

The key to the speed-power curve in the displacement mode is the Froude number, defined in the late nineteenth century by Englishman William Froude. From a number of tests performed in the 1890s on thin planks, Froude discovered that a boat's speed tops out when the wave it is creating has the same length as the boat's waterline. At this point a single wave stretches from the bow of the boat to the stern, and the bow trims upward as the forward part of the hull attempts to climb the bow wave. At this speed, further

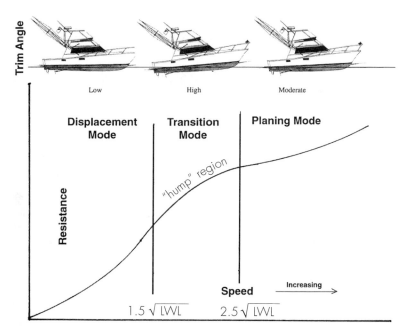

The speed-power curve shows how much resistance a boat generates as speed increases. As a boat's speed increases in displacement mode, the bow trims up and the stern squats. At a speed roughly equal to 1.5 times the waterline length, if the hull is designed to plane, it will move into a transitional region where it is neither planing nor operating in the displacement condition. In this semidisplacement, *semiplaning*, or hump region, the boat will have pronounced bow-up trim. When it breaks through the hump to a true plane, its speed increases, trim levels out, and engine power often can be throttled back.

application of power to a displacement hull becomes counterproductive, only causing the stern to squat and the boat to strain, for the bow wave is too steep for the hull to climb. In theory, this "hull speed," in knots, is $1.34\sqrt{LWL}$, which is the Froude number. In practice, because most boats have a little bit of overhang and are often slightly overpowered, we can assume that the typical maximum speed of a displacement hull is about $1.5\sqrt{LWL}$.

Above that speed lies the "hump" region, the fuzzy transition from displacement to planing mode. When a planing hull is accelerating through the hump region, the bow trims upward (the trim angle may get as high as 7–10 degrees), the stern squats in the wave trough, and the engine must run at high revolutions (rpm) as the boat tries to break free of the displacement condition. Through this transition the resistance of the hull increases more quickly than speed, but at the top

end of the transition—at a speed of 2.5 to $5\sqrt{LWL}$ or even higher—the boat is finally over the "hump." The resistance curve flattens out. Less power is needed to stay on plane, because hydrodynamic lift supports much of the boat's weight, leaving less of the hull in contact with the water and reducing the wetted surface area. Usually the engine can be slightly throttled back. The trim angle decreases, and the boat's motion smoothes out. At this point the boat is truly planing and has successfully escaped the constrictions of Froude's law. Broadly speaking, a boat with enough bearing area aft and enough horsepower can rise up onto a plane. How a designer achieves that bearing aft is a subject we return to.

A boat designed for high-speed operation can operate in a displacement mode, of course (because few people care to dock or negotiate a crowded anchorage at planing speeds!), but the hull of a displacement boat cannot be powered to operate in

A Pro Air Nautique wakeboarding boat on a full plane at around 45 mph (72 kph). *(Correct Craft)*

planing mode. Increasing the power in a displacement hull eventually results in overpowering the hull. Once such a boat achieves hull speed, additional applications of power cause the stern wave to build until gravity causes it to collapse, creating a turbulent wake. At this point the boat squats, a condition in which the stern sinks lower and lower as more power is applied. Occasionally, squatting will create a stern wave so large that it breaks and rolls into the back of the boat, sinking it. In any case, fuel consumption is excessive.

In that twilight between planing and displacement hulls are semidisplacement or semiplaning boats. Neither fish nor fowl, these creatures of the hump region develop enough dynamic lift to help support the hull, but not enough to get up on a plane. Typically, a semiplaning hull at full speed trims up at the bow and drags a large stern wave. The powerboat world generally accepts that displacement hulls can not under any circumstances exceed 1.8

to $2.0 \sqrt{LWL}$, or 11 to 12 knots for a 36-foot (11 m) waterline.

OTHER DESIGN FACTORS

After speed, the other factors influencing design include seaworthiness, range, comfort, and cost. None of these factors can be taken out of context; each must be considered relative to the type of boat and its intended use. Nevertheless, it is instructive to imagine what a boat designed to optimize any one factor would look like.

SEAWORTHINESS

If we use seaworthiness as the defining parameter of selecting a powerboat, we would probably end up with a boat that looked like a U.S. Coast Guard rescue boat. The first feature that strikes you about these vessels is the relatively low freeboard and the high cabin. Both features serve a purpose. Low freeboard enables rescuers to easily drag people aboard the boat or to board other boats that may be sinking. The large-volume, watertight cabin helps the boat right itself should it capsize. Features like these are specific to lifeboats. The average recreational powerboat does not have a large-volume, watertight cabin and super-strong windows. And if it indeed has low freeboard, the reason may only be to allow crew to handle fish that are brought to the boat.

Like lifeboats, many commercial fishing boats also require low freeboard, in this case to handle pots and warps. Any deck that might get washed by heavy waves should be completely watertight, and the boat should have freeing or clearing ports—that is, openings in the side of the bulwark to let water flow off the deck through the side of the boat—or large scuppers.

A seaworthy boat then is a boat designed to operate most efficiently in the conditions in which it is expected to operate. For example, a boat designed for use on a small lake is unlikely to encounter large waves. A similar boat designed for use on the ocean might be considerably

heavier and stronger to head into gale-driven waves 30 feet (10 m) high.

Creating a seaworthy boat brings into play other factors besides freeboard and watertightness. Paramount to the person selling the boat are aesthetics. The most seaworthy boat in the world might not sell if it looks big and clunky. And because this boat is so seaworthy it might also be very expensive. For example, window glass on a 41-foot (12.5 m) lifeboat might be 1 inch (2.5 cm) thick, or even more, and be secured through the cabin side with a metal frame and bolts every 2 or 3 inches (5–7 cm). To put glass of this thickness in a recreational sportfishing boat is prohibitively expensive, and is not needed if the boat is used only on weekends and is unlikely to encounter severe weather.

Having decided that the boat should be seaworthy for the conditions under which it will operate, we then need to look at different types of boats and determine what seaworthy features they should have. The accompanying table starts this process, and chapter 7 discusses it in greater detail.

(continued on page 10)

U.S. Coast Guard rescue boats such as this 41-footer (12.5 m) are ruggedly built and have low freeboard to help get people aboard from the water. *(U.S. Coast Guard)*

Seaworthiness Factors

Hull Shape	Most Efficient Hull	Fastest Hull	Inshore Fishing	Water Skiing	Wake Boarding	Trawler-Style Yacht
Boat speed	low to moderate	highest	low to moderate	high	high	low
Sea states	flat water	flat water	moderate seas	flat water	moderate waves	moderate to large seas
Wave height	0–1 feet	none	0–2 feet	0–1 feet	up to 3 feet	sea heights to 30% of length
Hull shape	round hull	3-point hydro	V or round	V hull	V hull	round or V
Hull length	long	moderate	moderate seas	moderate	moderate waves	moderate to long
Draft	shallow	low	shallow	shallow	moderate to deep	moderate to deep
Waterline length	long	low	moderate	moderate	moderate to heavy	moderate to heavy
Beam	narrow	wide for stability	moderate	proportional to length	proportional to length	proportional to length
Displacement	light	as light as possible	light to medium	moderate to light	moderate to heavy	moderate to heavy
Horsepower	low or very low	very high	low to moderate	high for length	high for length	low to moderate
Bow height	low to moderate	low	low to moderate	low to moderate	low to moderate	high
Bow fineness	fine to moderate	fine	fine to moderate	moderate	moderate	moderate to full
Bow flare	moderate	none	minimal	minimal	moderate	moderate to high
Deadrise angle	low	moderate	0–5 degrees	0–5 degrees	5–10 degrees	5–12 degrees
Sea-worthiness	limited	limited	limited	limited	limited	good
Comfort when stopped	tendency to roll	none	moderate	moderate	moderate	some roll
Comfort at cruising speed	comfortable	none	moderate	moderate	moderate	comfortable
Comfort at full speed	comfortable	none	moderate	moderate	moderate	comfortable
Range	moderate	limited	limited	limited	limited	extensive
Construction costs	moderate to high	very high	moderate	moderate to high	moderate	moderate to high
Suitable for use on:						
Estuaries/ salt marshes	yes	no	yes	no	no	no
Small ponds/ small lakes	yes	no	yes	yes	yes	yes
Large lakes	select optimum conditions	select optimum conditions	select optimum conditions	select optimum conditions	select optimum conditions	yes
Coastal shorelines	select optimum conditions	select optimum conditions	select optimum conditions	select optimum conditions	select optimum conditions	yes
Open ocean	select optimum conditions	no	select optimum conditions	select optimum conditions	select optimum conditions	select optimum conditions

Inshore Cruiser	Offshore Cruiser	Offshore Sport-fisherman	Inshore Racer	Offshore Racer	Inshore Catamaran	Offshore Catamaran
moderate	moderate	high	very high	very high	moderate to high	very high
moderate to large seas	moderate to large seas	moderate to large seas	moderate seas	moderate to large seas	moderate seas	moderate to large seas
sea heights to 20% of length	sea heights to 30% of length	sea heights to 30% of length	sea heights to 20% of length	sea heights to 30% of length	sea heights to 20% of length	sea heights to 30% of length
round or V	round or V	V hull	V hull	V hull or catamaran	round or V	mostly V
moderate to long	moderate to long	moderate	long	long	long	long
moderate to deep	moderate to deep	moderate	low to moderate	low to moderate	low	low
moderate	moderate to heavy	moderate	long	long	long	long
proportional to length	proportional to length	proportional to length	proportional to length	narrow for length	narrow hulls/ wide overall	narrow hulls/ wide overall
moderate to heavy	moderate to heavy	moderate	light to moderate	light to moderate	low to moderate	light to moderate
low to moderate	moderate	moderate to high	high	high	moderate to high	moderate to high
low to moderate	high	moderate to high	low	low	moderate	moderate
moderate to full	moderate to full	moderate	fine to moderate	fine to moderate	moderate	moderate
low to moderate	low to moderate	high	minimum	minimum	moderate	moderate
5–12 degrees	8–15 degrees	10–18 degrees	8–20 degrees	15–25 degrees	10–20 degrees	15–25 degrees
good	excellent	good to excellent	limited	moderate to excellent	good	good
some roll	some roll	good	some roll	some roll	good	good
good	excellent	good to excellent	good	moderate	good	good
good	excellent	good to excellent	good	good	good	good
moderate	extensive	good	limited	good	low to moderate	high
moderate	moderate to high	moderate to high	high	moderate to high	moderate to high	moderate to high
yes	no	no	no	no	no	no
yes	yes	yes	no	no	yes	no
select optimum conditions	yes	yes	yes	yes	yes	yes
select optimum conditions	yes	yes	yes	yes	yes	yes
select optimum conditions	yes	yes	select best conditions	yes	select optimum conditions	yes

RANGE

A boat's range (how far it can go on one tank of fuel) also is predicated on the speed at which the boat moves. A boat moving slowly, say at 10 knots, will use less fuel than the same boat moving at 30 knots; consequently, the slower boat's range will be larger even though it will take longer. Range also depends on the wind and sea conditions in which the boat operates, the efficiency of the hull shape, the efficiency of the drive train (engine, transmission, shaft, and propeller), and the weight of cargo as well as the number of people on board.

If we want to design a boat for maximum range, we must first make the hull efficient for the speed at which it is to run. Efficient hulls tend to be light, long, and narrow, rather like a kayak or an eight-person rowing shell. A long and narrow boat powered by a small engine moves easily through the water. Depending on the capacity of its fuel tank, such a boat may have an extraordinary range, but it is easy to capsize and its accommodations are limited. Long, light boats were common in the late 1800s. In the United States, they sliced the waters of Long Island Sound in service as commuter launches, taking financiers from their New York and Connecticut homes to Wall Street offices. The steam engines of the day couldn't generate enough power to lift a hull out of displacement mode, so the most feasible way to increase speed was to increase the waterline length of a narrow hull. But those splendid splinters capsized occasionally. A modern variant is the trimaran's long narrow center hull with two supporting floats to reduce the risk of capsizing.

Accommodations are difficult to fit into a narrow hull. Even on the trimaran variant, the necessity for light weight reduces the amount of gear on board as well as the comfort level.

The weight of gear and provisions required for longer range cruising requires more power and a somewhat less efficient hull. Because the crew will be aboard for a longer time, going farther also requires more comforts. And because the boat will be at sea longer, it is more likely to encounter bad weather; therefore it will need to be more seaworthy and of stronger construction. Taken together, these considerations lead to a heavier, more strongly constructed hull. Also, because it is not desirable to have a hull that may capsize easily, the hull will be beamier. Instead of a sleek, fuel-efficient, low-powered hull, we end up with a wider, more heavily powered, stronger, and more seaworthy cruiser with a wide range.

Thus, although a designer finds it fun to design a single-use boat, trade-offs often dictate heavier power and more equipment, more beam, and stronger construction than the original design brief. But that is the nature of design compromise.

COMFORT

If you had to design the most comfortable boat in the world, what would it look like? How fast would it go? And where would you take it? Comfort is related to speed. If you go slowly, you'll have a less bumpy ride. An English canal boat, for example, has all the comforts of a land home and proceeds at about 2 to 4 knots on serene waterways with few waves. If you want to go farther afield—let's say into the open ocean—your boat may be equally as comfortable when docked, but

A **V**-hulled coastal cruising boat will typically have high freeboard for cabin headroom, especially forward, as in this Wellcraft 350 Coastal. (*Wellcraft Marine*)

underway the ride is likely to be bumpier as the boat encounters waves and wind. The action of the sea on your boat will be different than in the canals of England and will require a different hull shape. The coastal cruising hull might be slightly faster—up to 18 knots—and it will have higher freeboard, a pointed bow, possibly a round hull or even a V-hull shape, and larger engines. In common with the canal boat it will have a moderately heavy displacement, or weight, unless it has been designed from ultralight (and ultraexpensive) materials. Chapter 8 looks at comfort in more detail.

COST

Boats are expensive. A small boat with an inboard engine can cost as much as a car. A larger boat prepared to go offshore or cross an ocean can cost more than most people earn in a lifetime. At the least expensive end of the production-boat spectrum you can find a boat assembled with a chopper gun or rotomolded (see chapter 12, How a Boat Is Built) and sold in mall retail outlets. Such a boat is made from one or two molded parts and is intended for fishing or recreation close to shorelines. Building it requires only a few hundred dollars' worth

The Wellcraft 8300 Martinique is a reasonably priced sport cruiser that sleeps six in three separate cabins. (*Wellcraft Marine*)

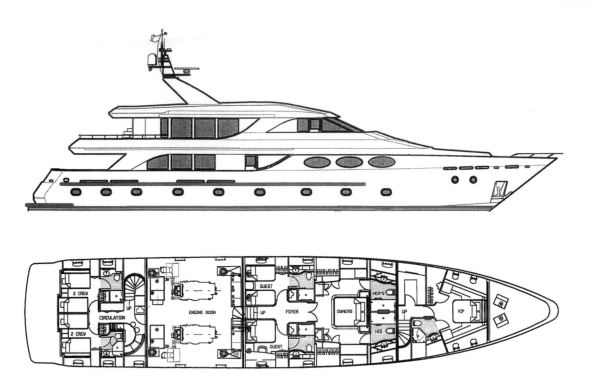

The profile and interior layout of a 120-foot (36.6 m) motor yacht. This boat qualifies as a megayacht (90–140 ft./27.5–42.7 m) and would cost millions of dollars to purchase and hundreds of thousands more to maintain and operate each year. A superyacht (longer than 140 ft.) would be even more expensive. But it will take you anywhere in the world in extraordinary comfort. *(Intermarine Savannah)*

of fiberglass and resin or other plastic, and about 4 to 8 hours of labor—often supplied in nonindustrialized countries where labor rates are low.

As the boat grows in size and comfort, not only does the initial purchase price increase—geometrically with length—but the operating costs increase, as well. The annual *operating* expenses for a large yacht run the *purchase* price of a smaller boat. For example, just painting the exterior of a superyacht may cost over a hundred thousand dollars—and boats like this are painted every few years. In addition to painting the hull, the vessel may have three to five professional crew and may

take over 1,000 gallons (3,785 L) of fuel every time its tanks are filled.

Initial costs include the materials and labor of building, the cost of outfitting, and the costs of loan origination. Typically, material costs are about half of the total. A rough estimate is that the hull and deck cost about 25 to 28 percent of the total boat, with the balance attributed to engine, tanks, props, hardware, etc.

Operating costs include paying the crew, transit and port fees, fuel costs, food and maintenance, and insurance. These costs can run between 5 to 20 percent of the overall cost of the boat annually, depending on where it will sail.

2

THE LANGUAGE OF HULL SHAPES

HAVING TOUCHED ON the requirements of the displacement, semidisplacement, and planing operating modes, we're ready to see how these requirements influence hull shape. Under each of the three major design types we examine the effects of desired seaworthiness, operating range, comfort, and cost. First, though, it will be helpful to define the terms and views by which powerboat designs are understood.

READING THE LINES

The best way of beginning that process is by reference to a lines plan drawing like the two on these pages. Each one shows three views: a *profile* of the hull as seen from the side, a *plan view* of the boat as seen from above, and a view from in front of or behind the boat. Together these three drawings define the shape of the boat.

PROFILE VIEW

In the profile view, the outline shows the shape of the boat at its longitudinal center-line. But that's only part of the story—it fails to convey the fore-and-aft shape of the boat at other points between its centerline and point of maximum beam. To address this, vertical cuts are made through the hull, parallel with the centerline and at 6- to 12-inch (15–30 cm) intervals outward, rather like a loaf of bread sliced lengthwise. The lines described on the hull surface by these cuts are known as *buttock lines*, and their shapes offer a clue to the boat's performance potential. In a high-speed planing boat, the buttocks will run straight aft from about the midsection, whereas in a slow-speed displacement hull they may turn upward fairly steeply aft.

The profile view also is cut horizontally by waterlines that parallel the boat's design waterline. These cuts, too, are spaced between 6 and 12 inches (15–30 cm) apart, and the waterplanes they describe can be seen clearly in the plan view.

PLAN VIEW

From the waterplanes in the plan view, you can get a feel for how the hull changes from the keel to the sheerline, where the

(continued on page 18)

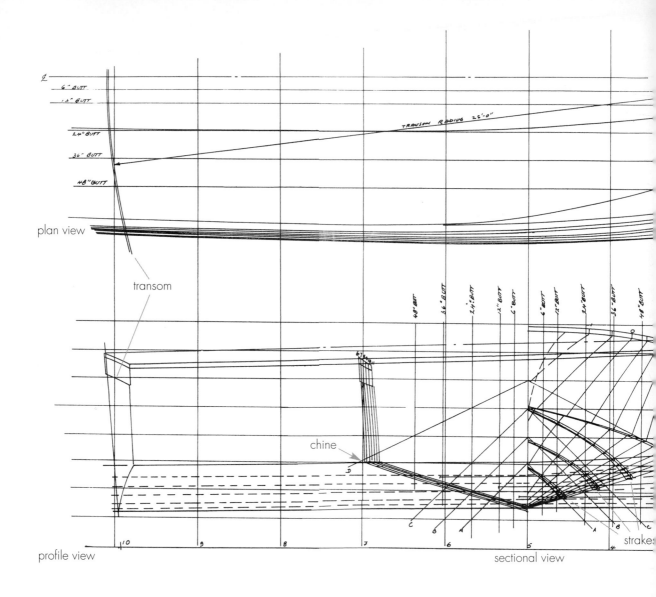

plan view

transom

chine

strake

profile view

sectional view

A set of lines for a moderately **V**-hulled boat. This hull will reach semidisplacement or plan-ing speeds, depending on the power package. The sectional view (in the middle of the profile at the bottom) clearly shows the chine, or sharp corner where the bottom meets the topsides. Visible at station 5 (the widest section) is a shelf, or *chine flat*, between bottom and topsides, which provides hydrodynamic lift. The angle of rise in the bottom sections rel-ative to the horizontal, known as *deadrise*, is constant from the midsection aft, making this a constant-deadrise hull. Note the longitudinal ribs visible on the bottom over the forward sections. These *strakes*, like the chine flat, provide additional lift. The bow sections are not deeply V'd, indicating that the boat may pound a little in a seaway but has ample room for accommodations forward.

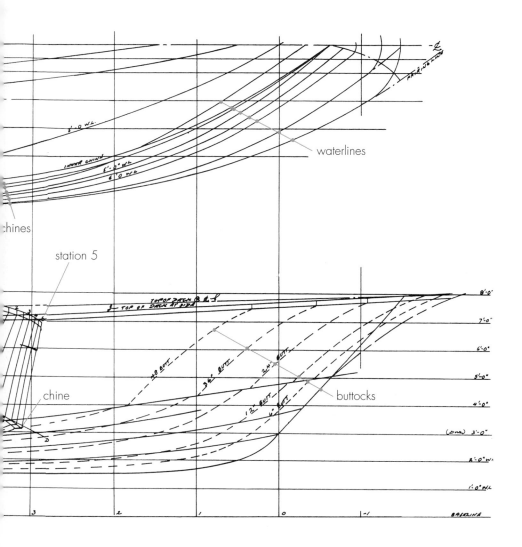

waterlines

chines

station 5

chine

buttocks

In the profile view the buttock lines (dashed) change direction abruptly where they cross the chine, then run out straight and flat aft, indicating that this hull has enough bearing aft to plane. The lifting strake centerlines are shown on the profile view as solid lines running from the bow and ending just aft of station 5. Above the profile and section views is the plan view, which shows the waterplanes of the hull at 12-inch (0.348 m) vertical intervals. The bow sections are *flared*—that is, the topsides forward curve outward as they rise—which provides reserve buoyancy in a head or following sea and also helps keep spray off the deck. Note how the bow is faired in both plan and profile to imaginary lines beyond the actual bow, then rounded off.

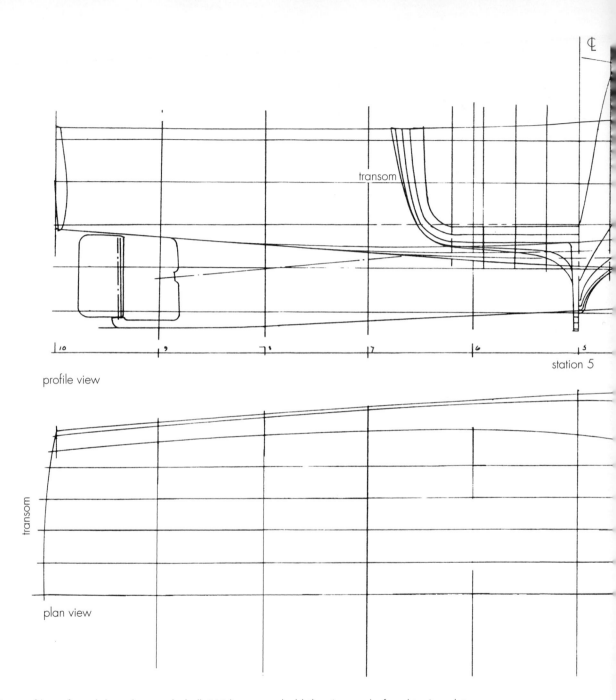

transom

station 5

profile view

transom

plan view

A set of lines for a lobster-boat-style hull. With its rounded bilge (instead of a chine) and its keel for strength, directional stability, and to protect the running gear, this is not an efficient planing hull. Yet its flat sections aft provide a lot of bearing, and it can get on plane given sufficient power and good weight distribution. Because of the upward slope of the afterbody in profile, the boat may trim up by the bow considerably as it gets onto a plane. To

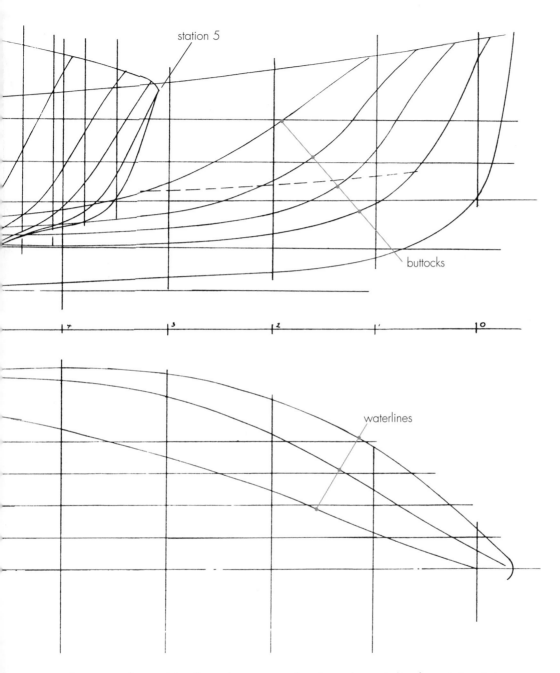

station 5

buttocks

waterlines

reduce spray forward it will need a spray strake above the waterline from station 1 to about station 4 (shown by dashed line). You'll have to slow down in a following sea or those deep bow sections will dig into the backs of waves and cause you to *broach*, or slew around broadside to the seas.

On slower hulls *(upper right)* water flow tends to follow the buttock lines, rising up the stern until gravity makes it fall. This effectively limits the speed at which the boat can travel. At slow speeds the boat slips cleanly through the water, but when pushed at higher than displacement speeds the stern tends to sink down in the water (a condition known as *squat*), and the stern wave becomes huge. If the boat is pushed even harder, the stern wave could break into the stern and flood the boat. A planing hull *(lower right)* features flat buttock lines aft and a squared-off transom to achieve clean wake separation at high speed, though the immersed transom and full stern sections make it inefficient at displacement speeds.

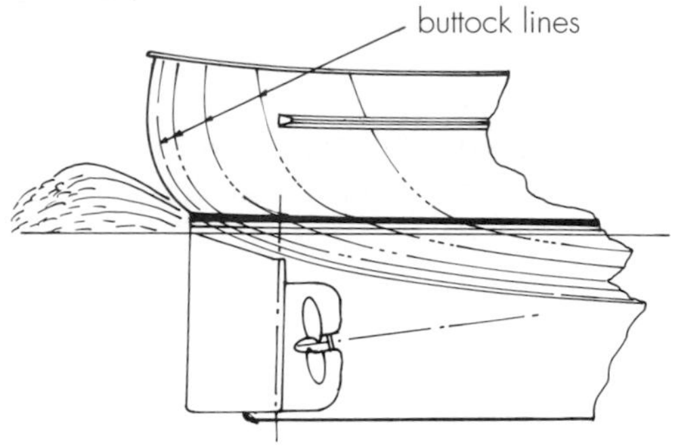

buttock lines

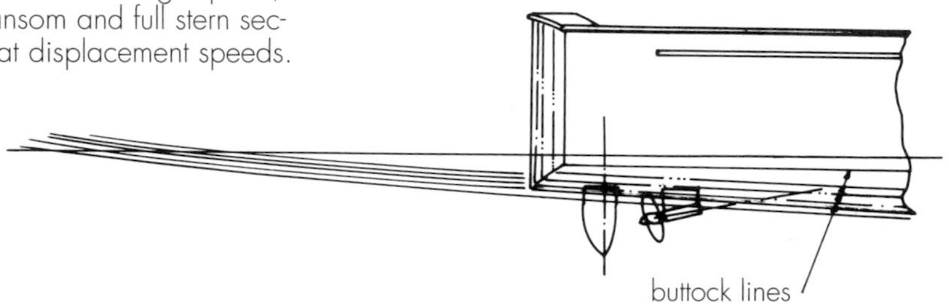

buttock lines

(continued from page 13)
hull sides meet the deck and superstructures. If the buttock lines curve sharply upward in the profile view, the plan view reveals that the waterplanes aft are pinched and narrow. Again, these are sure indications of a displacement hull that lacks sufficient bearing aft to climb onto a plane. A chine hull (see below) usually has a jog in its waterlines that gives away the chine's location.

SECTIONAL VIEW

In both the profile and plan views, the boat is further subdivided into stations perpendicular to the waterlines (profile view) and the fore-and-aft centerline (plan view)—the latter is like a sliced loaf of bread. Usually a boat has ten such stations, although some designers use more, and others fewer. Viewing the sections from the bow or stern brings them to life. Generally, the five forward stations are displayed on the right-hand side of the drawing, and the five after sections are on the left-hand side. In this view you can see at a glance whether you're looking at a deep-V, shallow-V, or round-bilge hull. You can tell how much volume and bearing there is aft, how sharp is the boat's entry, and how the deadrise varies from the entry to the transom. These terms will be defined as we go along; suffice it to say that the sectional view carries a wealth of information. In particular, the midbody or midsection shape (typically the shape at section 5) defines the shape of the entire hull and helps to define the displacement and stability of the boat.

Today, however, you rarely see lines plans displayed like this; these drawings are a relic of the drafting board. Almost all designers now draw their lines plans on a computer, using programs such as Nautilus (from New Wave Systems, Jamestown, Rhode Island), Multisurf (from Aero-

Hydro Inc., Southwest Harbor, Maine), MacSurf for Macintosh computers, or Vacanti Software (Renton, Washington). These computer programs organize the various views much differently, and often now in 3-D. In addition, they calculate displacement, hydrodynamics, and more, all with the push of a couple of buttons, saving hours of manual calculations of areas and volumes. The calculations also can include a complete per formance prediction made in minutes, a preferable alternative to waiting for the boat to be launched to find out how it will perform.

FEATURES OF HULL DESIGN

A few features of powerboat hull design are so common that it's hard to discuss powerboats without mentioning them. We take a quick look at those features here and develop them further later in the book.

CHINES

Look at many powerboats from the front or back, with the boat out of water, and you'll see a more-or-less sharp corner on either side where the hull bottom meets the sides. This is a *chine*. Chines usually run from bow to stern, curving upward at the bow and disappearing underwater near the middle of the boat. Chines can be hard (angular), soft (rounded), or reverse. A hard chine is typically seen on a semiplaning or planing boat and is intended to throw spray to the sides of the hull and prevent water from rising up the hull sides where it increases drag. Deep-V boats generally have wide flats at the chines to contribute additional lift.

Soft or rounded chines describe a sharp turn in the hull section but not a hard corner. For example, the hulls of some lobster boats feature soft chines. Soft chines give a smoother ride in a seaway than a hard chine, and a flatter bottom with higher speed potential than a round-bilge displacement design, but their top speed is

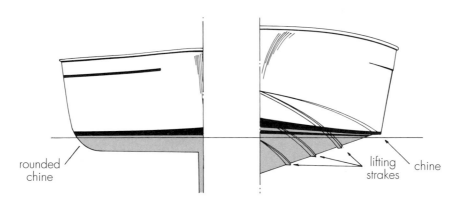

rounded chine

lifting strakes chine

Left: A soft chine is used on lobster-boat-style hulls, among others, and is much more tightly radiused than the gently rounded bilge of a displacement boat. It gives a softer ride than a hard chine, but still permits enough bearing area aft for planing. **Right:** A hard-chine hull has a flat or V bottom. The chine helps break water suction and provide clean separation when the bottom is rising on plane. Often, as here, it incorporates a chine flat for additional lift.

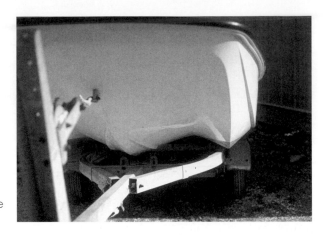

A Boston Whaler on a trailer, showing the cathedral hull form.

not as high as a hard chine. Often a boat with soft chines will have spray rails forward to break the suction of waves climbing the bow.

When viewed in section, reverse chines actually turn downward toward the water surface. The ultimate in a reverse-chine hull is a Boston Whaler, in which the chines form "tunnels" on either side. When the boat is underway, water thrown out by the center hull is deflected downward by the reverse chines to provide additional lift. This hull shape is often known as a *cathedral hull* because the tunnels on either side of the main hull look like mini-cathedrals.

DEADRISE

Deadrise is the angle a hull bottom makes with the horizontal plane when viewed from ahead or astern. The right amount of deadrise gives a boat directional stability, a softer ride, and reduces wetted surface drag as the boat rises onto plane. Deadrise is said to be constant if it stays approximately the same from the middle of the hull to the transom; it is variable if it changes from a deep angle at the mid-

section to a shallow angle at the transom. Deep-V hulls tend to have constant deadrise, but variable-deadrise hulls are thought to give a smoother ride at moderate speeds in a seaway for the same or less horsepower than a deep-V. The variable-deadrise hull is sharper forward and hits the water more softly, while aft it is flatter, which limits squatting and provides more bearing for climbing onto a plane. But at offshore racing speeds, when so much of the hull is out of the water that the aft sections rather than the forward sections meet the waves, the V'd hull is the hull of choice.

In general, the deadrise angle determines at what speed and sea state a planing boat can best power. Imagine a butter knife. If you press the flat of the blade down into the butter, butter mashes out everywhere, but the sharp edge cuts easily. Similarly, a flat-bottomed boat mashes water everywhere, whereas a high-deadrise hull tends to cut into the water until the hull volume slows the downward impetus and softens the ride.

A flat-bottomed boat (with 0 deadrise) pounds heavily in a seaway, making the ride very uncomfortable at any planing

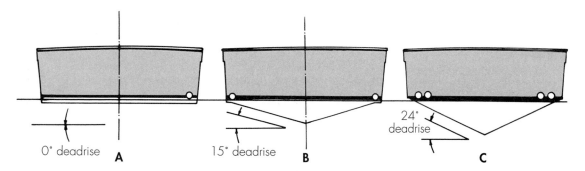

When only one deadrise angle is given in the specs for a boat, it is usually measured at the transom. In general, the higher the deadrise angle, the softer the ride and the faster the boat can be operated in a seaway. **A** shows a hull for use in flat water. The general-purpose hull shape in **B** has a 15-degree deadrise for use in moderate waves. **C** is a deep-V hull that might be used on a high-speed offshore boat. A flat-bottomed boat can get on a plane easily because the entire bottom surface contributes to the hull lift. Introducing deadrise makes it harder for a boat to get on plane because only a component of the hull forces (acting at right angles to the hull) are contributing lift. Strakes are used on deep-V hulls to give extra lift. The difficulty of getting on plane causes increased drag, which in turn increases fuel consumption for the same engine horsepower.

speed. Ask any fisherman who uses a flat-bottomed clam skiff. But the same boat powering across a flat-calm harbor would provide a very comfortable, stable ride. This suggests that the sea state in which you are going to cruise should dictate the type of planing hull you choose. If you typically power across a lake in an early morning calm, you will get a faster and perfectly smooth ride in a flat-bottomed hull or one with 0 to 5 degrees of deadrise. If you boat near a shoreline where waves don't get very high, a deadrise angle of 5 to 10 degrees will be about right. If you must power into a heavy head sea on a regular basis, you should consider a deeper V hull with a deadrise angle of 15 to 24 degrees.

FREEBOARD

Freeboard is the distance from the waterline to the deck at the hull side. The freeboard

on a powerboat typically varies with the speed at which the boat operates. A powerboat intended for higher speeds will often show a reverse sheerline, with the highest freeboard near the midbody and the deck sloping down forward and aft. This is because the heaviest weights in the boat need to be aft (over the planing surface at high speed), which tends to trim the bow up at an angle when the boat is at rest. As speed increases, the bow trims up even farther until the boat gets onto a plane, at which point it levels off slightly. The high trim angles make it difficult to see over the bow, so the deck forward curves downward to increase visibility.

Fishing boats require low freeboard at the stern so an angler can reach the water's surface or a fish leader. Consequently, freeboard aft shouldn't exceed more than about 24 to 36 inches (61–91 cm), which on a larger boat often necessitates an abrupt dip in the sheerline.

Freeboard is the distance from the top of the deck at the side of the hull to the water surface. It is measured at the bow and at the stern, often at the stemhead and the corner of the transom.

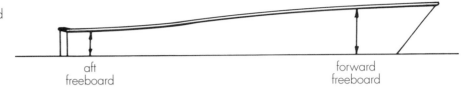

aft freeboard

forward freeboard

This 23-foot (7 m) Wellcraft Excalibur SCS shows reversed sheer—a slight downward turn in the freeboard forward to give better visibility as the boat gets on plane. *(Wellcraft Marine)*

The Luhrs 290 shows how freeboard is raised forward to help the boat power through waves. The pronounced flare in the bow sections also helps in this regard. Freeboard is much lower aft to enable a fisherman to reach the water's surface and handle fish. *(Luhrs Corp.)*

FLARE

When the hull of a boat gets progressively wider above the waterline, it is said to be *flared*. Semiplaning and sportfishing boats often have a flared bow so that when the bow is driven into a wave it has plenty of reserve buoyancy above the waterline. This flare is most extreme on boats that run the inlets along the Atlantic coast from the Carolinas to New Jersey, where breaking waves often pile up quite high.

KEELS AND BILGE KEELS

A centerline keel is used to give directional stability and to help limit rolling on displacement and some semidisplacement boats such as fishing boats, trawler yachts, and cruisers. Keels add a lot of drag to the hull and almost never appear on boats that

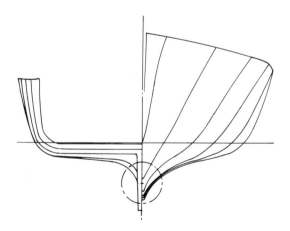

The sections through a lobster-boat-style hull (very similar to the one in the lines drawing on pages 16–17) clearly show the centerline keel. This keel is deep enough to protect the propeller (represented by the circle) when the boat is in the water.

move faster than 35 mph (56 kph). A centerline keel also protects the prop and rudder when the keel draft exceeds the draft of the running gear (struts, props, etc.).

On some displacement designs, bilge keels run along either side of the hull bottom near the turn of the bilge. In general, they are not very deep but often run about a fifth to a quarter of the length of the hull. At slow speeds they help stop the boat from rolling and provide some directional stability.

RUNNING STRAKES

Strakes provide additional lift for high-speed hulls. They are usually triangular in cross section with the bottom face parallel to the water surface, as shown in the accompanying illustration. They also create additional drag, so they usually end about one-half to two-thirds of the way aft. At one time strakes tended to be very narrow, but today designers make them a lot wider to more effectively increase lift as the boat moves onto a plane. Though fully immersed in displacement mode, the strakes provide lift and begin to emerge from the water at their forward ends as the boat's speed increases and it trims up by the bow. As the boat rises onto a plane, the uppermost strakes rise clear of the water, eliminating their lift but—more importantly at this point—also eliminating their drag. As speed continues to increase, the next pair of strakes rises clear of the water, and so on until the hull is running at maximum speed. At this point the hull may be riding only on the after portion of its bottom, with no strakes in the water.

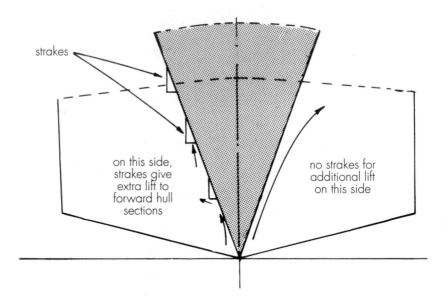

strakes

on this side, strakes give extra lift to forward hull sections

no strakes for additional lift on this side

Underwater portions of a bow and stern section of a hull with *(left)* and without *(right)* strakes. Running strakes help a hull generate dynamic lift and make it easier to get on a plane. They are usually located in the forward part of the boat and often end well in front of the transom.

TRIM ANGLE AND TRIM TABS

As a boat speeds up, it tends to trim up by the bow. This puts the hull bottom at an angle of incidence to the water passing beneath it that generates the necessary lift. As speed increases still further, trim may increase to an angle of about 7 to 10 degrees. A high trim angle makes it difficult to see other boats in front of you. When the boat moves onto a plane, trim angle decreases and the boat tends to level out.

Trim tabs can be used to adjust the trim

static waterline

trim angle

moving waterline

As a boat transitions onto a plane, the bow lifts and the stern sinks. The angle between the normal at-rest waterline and the waterline when the boat is underway is known as the **trim angle**.

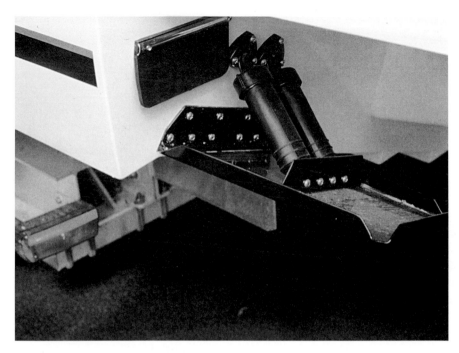

Trim tabs such as this one are fitted on both sides of the transom and are used to control the boat's attitude. They can also be used to "tilt" the boat slightly to leeward when high seas are coming over the weather bow.

angle to its optimum value for the prevailing speed. The tabs are usually fitted on the aft end of the hull and are adjusted using hydraulic rams. By angling the trim tabs downward as a boat accelerates, the boat can be popped onto a plane faster. Once the boat is planing, the tabs are readjusted for optimum trim.

3

HULL SHAPES

THE HULL OF A BOAT not only keeps the water out, it gives form and directional stability, aids seaworthiness, and is best shaped to suit the purpose of the vessel. Although virtually any hull can perform at displacement speeds, only specialized hulls can perform at high speeds, and only very specialized hulls can perform at ultra-high speeds. In this chapter we look at some of the standard shapes.

DISPLACEMENT HULLS

What is the best hull for a specific purpose? Often, especially for slower boats, there are several options. These shapes have evolved partly from evolution, partly from scientific testing, and partly from designers' intuition.

A displacement hull cannot escape its "hole in the water" to get up on a plane. It simply displaces the water in which it floats. Thus, a displacement hull never will be faster than its waterline length dictates. That limitation aside, however, displacement designs have a lot to offer: comfort, seaworthiness, range, load-carrying ability, fuel economy, and variety. Freed from the

hydrodynamic requirements of speed, displacement boats can take virtually any shape, from a heavily loaded barge with a rectangular box section to a long, lean, canoe-shaped electric-powered launch. A displacement boat can be round-bilged or chined; it can even have a deep-V hull, but it cannot generate enough lift from its hull and engine or engines to plane. Oil tankers, tugs, and many superyachts have displacement hulls. In the recreational boating world, the most popular displacement hull shapes are trawler-style yachts, displacement cruisers, and tug yachts (the distinction between the first two has all but disappeared).

TRAWLER YACHTS

Through the magic of market speak, the term *trawler yacht* has attached itself to almost any roomy, stable, slow-speed cruising powerboat, whether round-bilged or chined. However, many professional designers take issue with the term. As noted designer Chuck Neville says, the typical trawler yacht doesn't look like a fishing boat, nor does it drag a net, so why call it one? He's right, of course, but marketing people continue to call these boats *trawler yachts* because the term connotes the stately grace and staying power of a deep-sea trawler, even though large windows and top hamper (engine stacks, masts, dinghies stowed on the upper deck, and a high bridge deck are often collectively called *top hamper*) are hardly features of deep-sea trawlers.

Round-Bilge Trawlers

The accompanying illustration shows a common displacement hull shape. The boat is intended to move along at a speed of 8 to 10 knots, hence the beamy hull with its rounded, seaworthy ends. The hull looks like a fat canoe and will be driven by a single engine and a large-diameter, slow-turning propeller. This shape can head into a strong sea without shipping a lot of water, and when it runs before a large sea the waves will merely lift the canoe-style stern without trying to slam it around as might happen to a transom stern. This stern shape is common among North Sea trawlers, whose hulls are around 48 to 50 feet (14.6–15.3 m) long because that is the best length to handle the short, steep seas that prevail there.

When beam-on in a seaway, a canoe-stern cruiser will roll heavily, especially because it often carries a lot of equipment high in the boat. Consequently, the hull may have a large keel to help dampen rolling and protect the rudder. Some boats of this style also have bilge keels to help limit rolling at slower speeds.

The round-bilge, transom-stern hull shown next page and in chapter 2 is typically known as a *lobster boat style*. A small spray

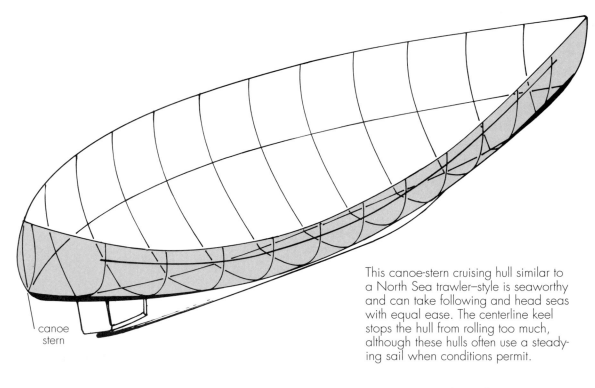

canoe stern

This canoe-stern cruising hull similar to a North Sea trawler–style is seaworthy and can take following and head seas with equal ease. The centerline keel stops the hull from rolling too much, although these hulls often use a steadying sail when conditions permit.

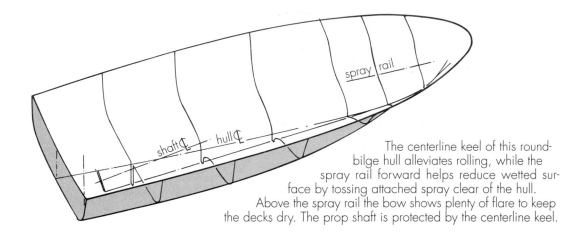

The centerline keel of this round-bilge hull alleviates rolling, while the spray rail forward helps reduce wetted surface by tossing attached spray clear of the hull. Above the spray rail the bow shows plenty of flare to keep the decks dry. The prop shaft is protected by the centerline keel.

rail forward breaks the suction between the water and the hull side. It has a bit of flare in its bow to make the anchor handling platform easy to use and to provide reserve buoyancy above the waterline. A long centerline keel leads back to the flat transom stern. This hull shape is great for inshore and coastal cruising, but I'm not sure I would like to be at sea in heavy weather in such a hull. Bashing into the wind and sea might be arduous because of the relatively low deadrise angle in the forward sections, while running off before a sea might force you to hand steer because an autopilot might not be able to prevent large seas from pushing the flat transom around.

Bow Sections The bow shape varies on a round-bilge hull. Many round hulls carry a spray rail at the bow to direct spray away from the deck, whereas others favor higher freeboard forward to keep seas off the deck and enable the boat to butt into a head sea.

Some trawler-style hulls feature bulbous bows, the idea being to flatten the bow wave—in effect creating a longer wavelength along the side of the hull—

thus lowering hull resistance and permitting a higher speed for the same horsepower. The bulb creates a wave of its own, the trough of which is supposed to coincide with and flatten the crest of the bow wave. Unfortunately, the ideal fore-and-aft position of the bow wave crest can only be obtained at one speed. Steaming at a higher or lower speed moves the bulb's wave trough away from the crest of the bow wave.

To find the optimum position, the hull should be tank-tested and the bulb optimized until it works properly at cruising speed. In boats where tank testing has been done the bulbs tend to be quite large. Most of the bulbous bows I have seen on trawler yachts appear too small to be effective. In one case, a boat was designed with a small bulb, but after tank testing and with the hull half-built, the bulb was enlarged. It then became so prominent that the anchor bounced off it when lowered, a problem solved by giving the yacht a clipper bow to move the anchor platform ahead of the bulb.

Another drawback of a bulbous bow is that it tends to increase the radius of the

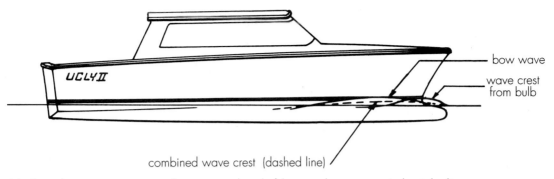

bow wave

wave crest from bulb

combined wave crest (dashed line)

A bulbous bow generates a small wave just ahead of the main bow wave. At the right displacement speed, ideally the designed cruising speed, the small wave reduces the height of the bow wave and therefore resistance. Going slower or faster reduces the bulb's effectiveness.

boat's turning circle. If you have to operate a trawler yacht routinely in tight quarters, look at one without a bulbous bow.

Moving aft from the bow, the lines of most round-bilge hulls widen quickly to maximum beam to enhance transverse (across the hull at right angles to the centerline) stability and load-carrying ability. Above the waterline, the bow sections of the canoe-stern hull on page 27 show virtually no flare, whereas the transom-stern hull opposite shows modest flare. Flare increases deck space and helps keep the deck free of spray when the boat is butting into a head or oblique sea. Either of the pictured hulls typically will have bulwarks forward that serve as an upward, above-deck extension of the hull sides. Bulwarks flaring upward from the deck enhance safety—as long as handholds can be placed in strategic locations—simply by making it very difficult to fall off the foredeck (my own experience shows, however, that you can sustain some nasty bruises!).

Some trawler-style hulls show an abrupt change in hull shape above the deck line, and on one production hull viewed in profile the bow actually turns back upon itself.

This "knuckle" has no obvious function and is probably a stylistic imitation of tugboat bows, where the knuckle protects the tug when pushing against a ship with a large overhang.

Midbody The midbody section defines the shape of the entire hull. A displacement hull is likely to have a rounded or a shallow-V midbody. All other things being equal, a rounded hull is more inclined to roll, but does so with an easier motion than a V hull. Increased beam tends to reduce rolling, as does a chine or bilge keel; however, both features increase wetted surface and drag, requiring slightly larger engines.

Stern The stern of a hull designed for maximum efficiency in the displacement mode is shaped to allow water to flow smoothly around the hull, thus minimizing unwanted turbulence in front of the propeller. A tapered stern—often seen on motorsailers and other low-powered vessels—is conducive to smooth water flow, whereas a transom stern promotes turbulence at displacement speeds. Old-time de-

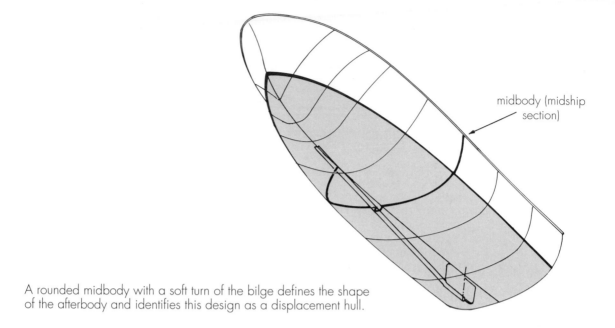

A rounded midbody with a soft turn of the bilge defines the shape of the afterbody and identifies this design as a displacement hull.

midbody (midship section)

signers recognized this fact, so they kept their hulls carefully streamlined below the waterline for the low-speed engines of the time. Typically, the stern on a low-powered hull is reminiscent of a sailboat stern.

In the drawings on pages 27 to 28 both hulls taper aft from amidships toward a clean stern allowing nonturbulent water to the propeller, though the canoe stern does this more successfully than the transom stern. A hull with a centerline keel requires a prop with an odd number of blades to eliminate the possibility of two blades being masked by the keel at any one time. If this were to happen, you would probably hear and feel vibrations throughout the boat.

Above the propeller, the hull shape usually follows the form dictated by the midship section; that is, a rounded midship section indicates a rounded hull aft. This is not always true, however; some hulls change from a rounded midsection to a chine just aft of amidships.

Freeboard High freeboard forward is useful for several reasons, first and foremost to keep the decks dry. When a boat butts into a head sea, spray and green water can come aboard over the bow. High freeboard minimizes this. When a boat rolls, high freeboard at the point of maximum beam keeps the deck edge out of the water longer, thus helping to prevent tripping on a sea. Finally, high freeboard increases headroom in the living and engine compartments. Note that the hull sides near the middle of both hulls shown on pages 27 to 28 are almost vertical. Flare in the midsection topsides is not needed and, in fact, can become a hindrance when docking because it blocks your view.

In the canoe-stern hull the deck curves slightly upward at the stern, again to minimize the amount of water coming aboard from astern when running downsea, and also to drain toward the midship *scuppers* (drains) any water that does come aboard.

Boats that run at the top end of the displacement mode often pull a large stern wave. Should this be reinforced by a large breaking wave overtaking from astern, the boat could get pooped—that is, swamped over the stern. For this reason alone it is worth slowing down when running downwind in heavy seas in a displacement hull.

Keels and Skegs Low-speed powerboats have none of the dynamic stability that planing or semiplaning powerboats do when running at speed. Consequently, they tend to roll in most sea states. A rounded hull is more likely to roll than a chined hull, but both types should have some form of keel to resist rolling. A centerline keel seems no more or less effective than bilge keels in this regard, but centerline keels are seen more often on chined hulls, and bilge keels on rounded hulls.

Instead of running a keel the entire length of the hull, some designers opt for a shorter skeg to protect the running gear without substantially increasing wetted surface area. This has the advantages of making the boat easier to turn relative to a long keel and slightly faster with modestly better fuel consumption.

V-Hull Displacement Cruisers

The accompanying illustration shows one of my designs, although the concept is similar to a Grand Banks–style cruiser. It has a V'd bottom with chine and an 8-degree deadrise angle, as shown in the sections. With its low-powered engines (twin 350 hp engines in a 54 ft./16.5 m hull), it will cruise at about 12 knots. Unlike the round-bilge displacement hulls shown above, this vessel could be fitted with larger engines to achieve a top speed of about 20 to 25 knots

and therefore could be classified with equal accuracy as a semidisplacement hull. Stated differently, this hull generates enough lift to reach semidisplacement speeds *if* (and it's a big if) it's given sufficient power. Because of its weight, however, it will not get onto a plane. Also, because of the low deadrise angle (especially at the bow), the hull might slam a little in a heavy sea.

Typically, because trawler-style V-bottom yachts don't require great seakeeping performance at high speeds, they have a constant deadrise angle and no chine flat (or at most a small one) at the edge of the chine. This type of hull does not need running strakes, since it does not have to generate lift. Freeboard is high simply to get headroom inside the hull, although it need not be quite as high when the cabin is slightly raised.

Bow Sections On chined hulls, the height of the chine gives an indication of the fineness (knife edge appearance) of the bow and the ability of the boat to meet head seas. If the chine runs fairly low at the bow, the bow sections form a shallow V with plenty of buoyancy to ride over low waves. Such a bow doesn't require much flare above the chine for reserve buoyancy, but shallow V sections forward make the bow slam and pound hard at higher speeds and in rough seas. A chine swept high at the bow makes the forward sections of the hull fine, and these highly V'd sections tend to cut through waves rather than bounce over them, making for a more comfortable ride in head seas. There comes a time, however, when the boat has to turn around and head downsea, at which time those fine bow sections dive into the back

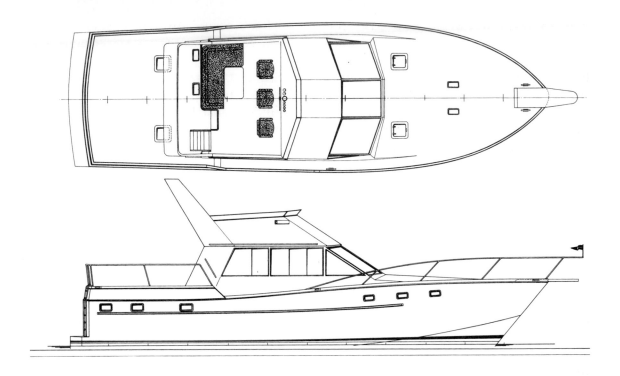

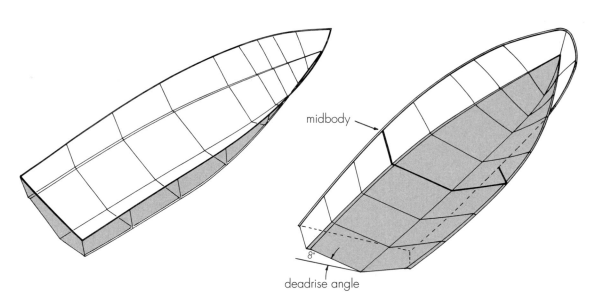

midbody

deadrise angle

8°

This 54-foot (16.5 m) power cruiser designed by the author is intended to cruise at 12+ knots. The sections show a narrow chine flat, though often a **V**-bottom power cruiser has none at all.

of every wave, often lifting the stern and leading to a potential broach. To counter this tendency, a boat with a deeply V'd bow usually carries a lot of flare above the chine to provide reserve buoyancy and to stop the bow from plunging deeply into waves. The designer's task is to find the compromise V shape that gives a good ride in both head and following seas—not so flat that it pounds, and not so fine that it digs and roots in the backs of following seas.

This trade-off also affects the interior accommodations forward. A deep-V hull has less interior volume than a shallow-V hull, possibly forcing the designer to shift the entire cabin arrangement slightly aft to make room for bunks in the forecabin. Ultimately, this affects the weight distribution and the engine and tank locations. One small design change can force other changes throughout the design.

The chine in the design on page 32 is carried to the stem to help break the suction of waves rising up the side of the hull. This not only helps to reduce overall hull resistance but also allows a slightly finer

angle of entry at the bow, yielding a softer ride in a head sea. Aft of the bow, the hull widens quickly to its maximum waterline beam to increase stability and keep the longitudinal center of buoyancy (LCB) well forward. Because the longitudinal center of gravity (LCG) must be over the LCB for a boat to trim level, keeping the LCB forward allows the designer to place the engines in the middle of the hull and fit an owner's stateroom aft. (On most powerboats, the combined weight of the engines and tanks comprises the greatest weight in the boat. These weights are moved forward or aft during the design phase to get a boat to trim level.)

This bow is not deeply V'd, since the boat is not intended to pound through heavy seas. The shallower V gives it a large forecabin and ample forward buoyancy to cope with following seas. A finer bow would move the hull's LCB farther aft, requiring the LCG (engines and tanks) to move farther aft, which would reduce space in the aft cabin.

The hull is not highly flared above the waterline, in keeping with the angular

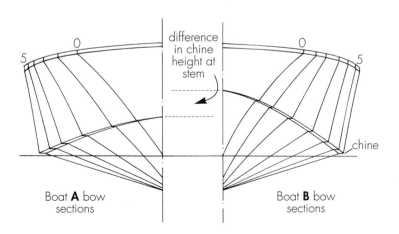

Boat **A** bow sections

Boat **B** bow sections

The height of the chine forward gives an idea of whether the bow will slam in a head sea. In **A** the chine is low and the **V** of the bow is fairly flat. This shape has plenty of buoyancy and volume in the forecabin, but it might pound in a seaway. In **B** the chine is much higher, making the **V** of the bow deeper. This shape will more easily cut into a head sea and is better in rougher water. The hull volume is less than in **A**, however, making the forecabin slightly narrower. On both boats the deck area and bow profile are the same.

look of the boat. Since the boat will be moving fairly slowly at full speed, there is no real need for a lot of flare.

The chine hull has a slightly harder ride with a little more stability than a round-bilge hull. In other words, it won't roll quite as much, but it will slam into heavy seas a bit more. (Slamming is relative. A boat moving at slow speed is unlikely to slam very hard, whereas a boat moving at high speed will often slam hard no matter what the hull shape.)

Stern On this 54-footer (16.5 m) the stern is chopped off rather abruptly. This is partly for styling reasons, but it also allows a boarding ladder to be placed aft, at the point of easiest access. A slight hull extension at the waterline allows the crew to board the boat easily from the dock and climb up the aft ladder. Below the waterline there is clean water to the props, but because of draft restrictions the hull has small tunnels in it to recess the props, thus reducing their overall depth. The skeg is minuscule, enabling the boat to turn quickly and easily.

SKINNY BOATS

According to Froude's law, the potential speed of a displacement hull increases with its waterline length. In displacement mode, a long boat will always go faster than a short one. Consequently, some yacht designers prefer long, slender boats to short, fat trawler-style yachts. In fact, slim hulls are more efficient throughout the speed range than their stouter counterparts. Consider the rowing shell, probably one of the skinniest boats ever built.

These craft, propelled by eight crew, have been clocked at around 14 mph (22 kph), and that is with eight crew—not horsepower.

Long, slim hulls require less power to drive, generally react better in a head or following sea, and unless the sea is coming from abeam they generally have a more comfortable motion than a fat planing hull. Considering that the fastest boat in the world in 1893 was the 100-foot-long, 8-foot-wide (30 by 2.4 m; length-to-beam ratio of 12.5) steam turbine-driven *Turbinia*, devotees of slim boats have a point. Many boats up to about the 1930s were long and narrow and routinely traveled at 30 to 35 knots with considerably fewer horses in the engine room than are used today. But most of these boats had a major drawback. Prop torque from the single propeller often caused them to heel up to 15 degrees when running at high speeds, and some even capsized.

The heeling problem can be largely alleviated by stabilizing the hull with amas, otherwise known as *outriggers*. Boats of this type routinely cruise at 20 to 30 knots with small engines and get remarkable efficiencies. The length-to-beam ratio of the main hull might be as high as 10 or 15 to 1, but the amas limit its rolling.

The remaining disadvantage of a very slim hull is the lack of accommodations. A long, narrow hull often looks like a train carriage with bunks on either side of a narrow walkway. Power trimarans have the same problem, because the accommodations are in the main hull and the amas are used solely for stability. In this case, the trade-off is space for efficiency, range, and high fuel economy.

The Transcat 48 is a comfortable cruising catamaran. *(The Catamaran Company)*

CATAMARANS

Another type of slim hull is that of the catamaran, which is made of two parallel hulls (amas or outriggers) that support an elevated bridge deck (aka or crossbeam). The length-to-beam ratio of each hull is around 6 or 8 to 1. This makes the hulls very efficient. With a main cabin over the bridge deck, a catamaran combines a huge amount of space with good fuel efficiency, lots of stability, and a relatively high speed.

I was never much interested in catamarans until I had a ride on a French-built Transcat 48. I was surprised by the smooth ride, the 22-knot top speed, and the generous bridge deck space. The hulls are V'd, with chines carried forward to the bow. Although it might not seem that there is much reserve buoyancy forward, waves never hit the bridge deck even at full speed. With an engine in each hull, maneuvering is remarkably simple.

This boat has three staterooms in the hulls, a large saloon with a dining area and galley, more dining space aft of the cabin, and a spacious bridge (we had ten people on the bridge, with room for more). Fuel consumption was a remarkable 10 gallons (37.9 L) per hour at 22 knots with twin 230 hp diesel engines. A catamaran like this makes sense if you're in the market for a 20-knot-plus cruiser. With two hulls, of course, it's expensive to build and thus to buy.

A small catamaran from Aquasport, the 161 Tournament Cat, provides a lot of stability and power in a small package. *(Aquasport)*

PLANING HULLS

A true planing hull uses hydrodynamic lift to rise up out of the water and reduce resistance. In order to plane, the hull must achieve an appropriate angle of incidence to the water flow, trimming up by the bow to generate lift. This is a similar lift principle that an airplane uses to get aloft. As the generated lift approaches the weight of the boat, the hull rises from the water and rides on top of the wave it creates.

The need to generate hydrodynamic lift places constraints on planing hull design such that all true planing monohulls share a number of features in common, including a chined hull with a deadrise angle that varies according to the design speed of the vessel. They often have lifting strakes along the hull that vary in length and placement according to the deadrise angle, and an abruptly cut-off transom (often called a *destroyer stern* in naval architecture) for good water separation. In other words, the transom meets the hull bottom at 90 degrees, and because water cannot turn at right angles when the boat is moving at speed, the water simply breaks free of the hull.

The hull may carry a constant deadrise angle from amidships aft, or it may have a warped, or *variable*, deadrise that gets progressively shallower from the midsection aft. The former is more likely on boats meant to carry their speed through almost any kind of seaway. A variable deadrise, on the other hand, combines sharp forward sections for reasonable seakeeping with flatter sections aft offering more interior room and more stability when drifting or running at displacement speeds. (A deep-V hull derives stability from dynamic lift at speed but is rolly when not planing.) On faster boats the forward part of the deck or sheer quite often slopes slightly downward. As mentioned earlier, this reverse sheer gives the operator good forward visibility while the boat is trimmed

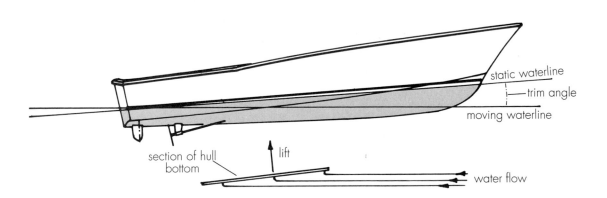

As speed increases, an appropriately shaped hull generates enough lift to rise onto a plane. Lift is generated by the action of water hitting the bottom of the hull while it is at an angle to the water flow, thus pushing the boat upward. Most of the hull rises out of the water until only about a third is immersed; this reduces wetted surface and allows the boat to travel faster with less power.

On the Cigarette Café 33 Open, the forward part of the deck turns downward to help increase visibility when the boat is trimmed bow up. *(Cigarette Racing Team Inc.)*

up by the bow during the transition from displacement mode to planing. Finally, most planing boats have a reasonably light displacement.

HIGH-SPEED DEEP-**V** HULLS

If you want to cruise fast in rough water, this is the hull form to choose. Deep-V hulls are so called because the deadrise angle is between 18 to 24 degrees at the transom. (If you ask about deadrise at a boat show you will always be given the angle at the transom, because designers armed with lines plans are the only ones who can find the deadrise at any other station.) Boats with high deadrise angles generally offer a "soft" ride but don't lift out of the water as easily to get onto a plane. To overcome this deficiency, strakes are used. These are generally triangular in cross section and run most of the length of the hull. For the same reason, some boats of this type have flat pads (an area about 6–8 in./15–20 cm wide and 36–48 in./91–122 cm long) on the aft end of the bottom centerlines of the V-shaped hull.

Deep-V hulls generally do not make good fishing platforms even though they can get to the grounds quickly. They tend to roll heavily when stopped, and because of the aft engine location they do not have a large cockpit area. The accompanying illustration shows the lines of a high-speed powerboat designed to operate at 60 knots plus. This hull has a deadrise angle of 22 degrees.

Bow

The bow of a high-speed boat can be recognized by its high chine and usually three, but up to five, strakes running aft. The hull sides are not flat but have a slight convexity (some have a slight concavity) to increase structural strength and to provide some reserve buoyancy in the event that they plow into a wave.

Midbody

The midbody of a high-speed boat for rough water is almost always a deep V. The deadrise angle may be quite high (above 22 degrees), depending on the speed at which the boat is to operate, and will be virtually constant from the midbody to the transom.

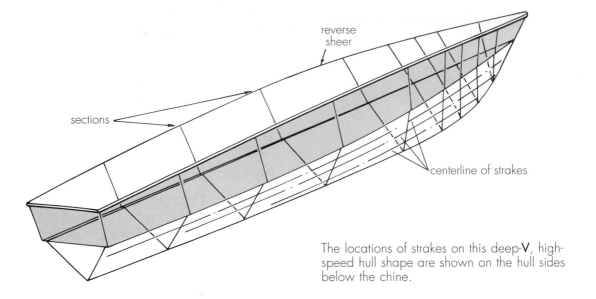

reverse sheer

sections

centerline of strakes

The locations of strakes on this deep-V, high-speed hull shape are shown on the hull sides below the chine.

Ski Boats

Ski boats are among the faster planing hulls, with relatively shallow deadrise (since a steeper V tends to create a larger wake) and a small fin amidships to increase lateral profile and make the boat steer better when towing a skier. The fin often looks like an inverted dolphin fin. The corners of the transom are rounded so that the chine wake rolls inward, flattening the wake crest. Ski boats also may have downward-turning chine rails or strakes to contain the wake and keep it flat, and the prop is set well forward so that its wake dissipates under the hull rather than popping up aft.

Wake-boarding boats differ from ski boats in that the wake needs to be huge to enable the wake-boarder to make jumps and do tricks. To accomplish this, wake-boarding boats force the stern down into the water to cause a pressure wave to pop out from under the boat. This means that many wake-boarding boats add ballast or locate tanks aft to get the stern down. A typical purpose-built wake-boarding boat might also have a deeper V hull than a ski boat to help generate a large wave crest. Other features that increase the size of the wake include trim flaps to push the stern wave down and make it pop up behind the boat, and placing the prop well aft so that the prop wake supplements the stern wave.

The 2000 Ski Nautique model with open bow. (Correct Craft)

Stern

The deep-V hull shown in the illustration opposite has flat buttock lines aft, in keeping with a quick jump onto a plane and extensive periods of running that way. The planing area is small and far aft on this boat, yet the boat's longitudinal center of gravity needs to be over the center of that waterplane. This means that the heaviest items on the boat, the main engines, are often located aft of the stationary center of buoyancy, giving the boat a pronounced bow-up trim at rest.

STEPPED HULLS

A further refinement of the deep-V hull is the stepped hull. Steps are breaks in the hull intended to reduce the amount of hull surface in contact with the water. Steps can run straight across the hull (although these are structurally weak and not often seen today), or they can be V-shaped, with the vertex facing forward or aft. They will have large apertures on the outboard side of the hull to allow air to be sucked down into and ventilate the step. In general, a speed increase of about 10 to 15 percent can be expected from a stepped hull over a nonstepped hull with the same power train. In a seaway, some stepped hulls may experience wave blockages of the step aperture on one side, leading to loss of lift on that side and throwing the boat into an unexpected turn. Stepped hulls should be used by experienced drivers who know what the hull is likely to do in a seaway and in hard cornering, and who know how to react to the unexpected.

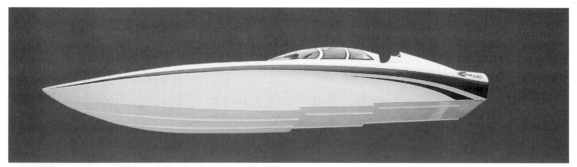

(Callan)

The Callan 55 shows twin-surface piercing props aft of twin trim tabs. *(Callan)*

FISHING HULL SHAPES

Fishing hull shapes tend to have quite specific requirements. Often they need to get to the fishing grounds quickly and then troll or power at very slow speeds. In other cases, certain types of hulls have been adapted for specific types of fishing.

SALTWATER FLATS BOATS

Flats boats, between 14 and 22 feet (4.3–6.7 m) long, are designed to be gently poled along while fishing in water between 1 and 3 feet (0.3–0.9 m) deep. They can easily cross a salt marsh, which are plentiful near fish spawning grounds. This shoal-water work necessitates a very different hull from fishing the offshore canyons. Flats boats have low freeboard that in any kind of seaway makes them extremely wet. If you have to cross an unprotected bay to fish a marsh, you may be

better off looking for a less restrictive vessel or trailering to an adjacent launching area.

If trailering is the option you choose, your boat must be easy to launch and recover, which translates into a reasonable weight and beam and a fairly light power package—although many flats boats use heavy 150 hp outboards. It also means that you should add the price of the trailer to your cost calculations.

The weight of a flats boat is critical. In general, the lighter the boat, the better it will run in shallow water without dragging a huge stern wave. Hull volume distribution is also critical. If the boat tips and bobs as you cast, you are likely to create pressure waves that will spook the fish long before your fly or bait arrives.

The ideal hull shape for crossing shallow water combines a deep-V entry with a moderate 5 to 7 degrees of transom deadrise.

The Wellcraft 270 Coastal Fisherman uses twin 250 hp outboards to drive its 7,253 pounds (3,290 kg). (Wellcraft Marine)

The Hells Bay Whipray 16, a flats boat, at planing speed just a few feet from the mangroves. Note the poling platform over the motor. (Hells Bay Boatworks)

An even more critical feature is how the boat performs when the engine is raised and the boat is poled along. Small wavelets slapping and resonating against the hull spook fish faster than tossing a rock. Many fishermen believe that there are good and bad hull slaps. One that sounds natural to a fish will not spook it; one that sounds unnatural will.

The deck needs to be a flat, uninterrupted working platform, preferably with lockers beneath it. After all, when you are poling the boat, you don't want to have to climb over thwarts and step across cleats and cockpit openings.

Another feature to look for is trim tabs. Putting tabs down when starting in shallows gets the boat on plane quicker, and the tabs also can be used to heel the boat when traversing a flat in a crosswind. Put the windward tab up and the leeward tab down to heel the boat slightly to leeward,

thus reducing the amount of spray coming aboard over the weather bow.

In their rush to respond to the current rage for flats boats, many manufacturers have adapted their bass boats for flats fishing. Often the hull shape of these converted designs is less than optimum, and the fishing suffers. When shopping for a flats boat, ask the experts. You'll find that the same manufacturers' names crop up again and again.

BASS BOATS

A friend of mine fishes for bass from a canoe. One summer he caught a 36-pound (16 kg) striped bass from it. "It took some fighting," he said over coffee, "but I finally landed it." The best angler can catch fish from any kind of boat, but for the rest of us, a purpose-built boat can be a big help. A bass boat doesn't have to go far offshore

The Alan Stinson–designed, 100 percent composite-hulled Stratos 21XL Magnum bass boat comes with a 250 hp Yamaha VMax and a Minn Kota trolling motor. (Stratos Boat Inc.)

and consequently doesn't need a lot of transom deadrise. About 5 to 10 degrees will do, depending on how rough the waters are where you fish. The bow needs to be moderately V'd to enable you to get to the fishing grounds quickly and to keep seas off the foredeck. The hull should be stable, and you should be able to walk around the boat without stepping over seats or tripping over gear. This makes center-console boats appealing.

OFFSHORE SPORTFISHING BOATS

The sportfishing boat hull needs to do several things well. It must run efficiently and quickly to the fishing grounds, drift or lie to an anchor while the anglers fish, and troll at a relatively slow speed (about 6 to 10 knots).

These requirements dictate the shape of the hull. Because it needs to get out to the fishing grounds fast, it will need to plane. Speeds of 30 to 40 knots often are required to get to the offshore canyons on a Friday afternoon. In order to generate the lift for planing, it should have a fair amount of beam, a V bottom, chine flats, and lifting strakes. If the boat will be going offshore, it should have a moderately deep deadrise aft in the range of 12 to 18 degrees. It will need a sharp entry to punch through a head sea. The boat should not roll too much while at anchor or adrift on the grounds or while trolling at slow speed in displacement mode. When the boat is stopped or trolling, the chine immerses to increase stability. The bow has plenty of freeboard and flare to prevent spray from coming aboard when the boat is en route to the fishing grounds. Because the helm-station is well up in the hull, there is no need to lower the sheerline forward as in a high-speed boat.

The Wellcraft 35 Scarab Sport is a fishing boat capable of 61 mph. It is powered by triple SX 250TXR2 Yamaha outboards that allow it to reach the fishing grounds quickly. (Wellcraft Marine)

SEMIPLANING OR TRANSITIONAL HULL SHAPES

Boats operating in the semiplaning, semi-displacement, or transitional mode usually carry a pronounced bow-up trim angle, have high fuel consumption, and leave a roiling wake behind them. To my mind, nobody should operate in the transitional mode, but designer Chuck Neville points out that the capability of doing so on rare occasions has value. "Most of my designs of this type," he says, "operate at slower speeds 95 percent of the time and are very efficient there. But the owner-operator has the capability of pushing the boat from, say 9.5 knots to 14 knots should the occasion demand it. This can spell the difference between making a safe haven before nightfall or ahead of a storm. There is certainly a price to pay in comfort and cost, but it is a trade-off that many owners are happy to make when the situation warrants." Note that engine manufacturers strongly recommend against running a large, high-revving engine at slow speeds for prolonged periods of time. In other words, if your engine is big enough to push your boat at 14 knots, you need to let it do that every now and then.

Boats operating in the transitional mode often are designed as planing boats but are underpowered or were built more heavily than the designer anticipated. Extra weight and/or less power prevents these hulls from getting over the hump (see chapter 1) and onto a plane. If you are the owner of such a boat and prefer to operate on a plane with the throttles open but cannot get over the transitional hump, look into reducing weight onboard, changing props (see chapter 10), or retrofitting more powerful engines. Modern engines are both lighter and more powerful than their predecessors. Often though, a builder might feel that a boat will give too hard a ride in the planing mode; to get an easier ride, he will power it for semiplaning speed.

Boats operating in the transitional regime can be either round-bottom (with a tightly rounded chine) or hard-chined in the manner of true planing hulls. Round-

The semidisplacement Sabreline 43 at speed. Note the pronounced bow-up trim, the forefoot almost out of the water, and the bow wave breaking away from the hull at the chine. This moderately heavy boat with V'd hull and 14 degrees of deadrise will achieve 18 to 20 knots. (Sabre Yachts)

bilge hulls such as those seen on Maine lobster boat types have enough flat surface aft to provide bearing for lift, which means the turn of the bilge must be tight (that is, the hull sides must turn upward fairly sharply) to keep beam within reasonable bounds. Chined hulls have a V bottom with deadrise angles up to 12 degrees, a chine flat, and a certain amount of flare forward over a relatively fine entry.

Most sportfishing and lobster-style boats plane fully or at least partially when lightly loaded. That is, they use dynamic lift to raise the boat up out of the water. When a boat is fully on plane, only a small part (the aft third) of the boat remains in the water, but when the boat is semiplaning, most of the waterline is immersed and the hull trims bow-up. (Note that, knot-for-knot, planing is more fuel-efficient than semiplaning, since it reduces the wetted surface of the boat. A boat that is planing can go faster with the same horsepower or farther at reduced horsepower than a boat that is semiplaning.)

BOW

Semiplaning boats incorporate various features forward to make them more efficient. A V-shaped bow with a high deadrise angle gives them the ability to meet a wave head on and not stop dead. Flare above the waterline throws spray to the side rather than conducting it aboard. A chine or strake forward breaks the suction between the bow wave and hull, reducing wetted surface and promoting lift. Slightly farther aft, the chine helps to keep spray away from the hull, while chine flats often provide additional lift. All these features help to keep the boat on a half-plane and give it a good ride in most sea states.

MIDBODY

As in a displacement hull, the midbody section can be round or V-shaped. A rounded

The spray rail is extra large on the Jamestown (Rhode Island) Fire Department's rescue boat to deflect spray and help keep the bow from burying. This is a semidisplacement boat—too heavy to really get up and go.

hull is advantageous in heavier seas. If V'd, the hull will need more deadrise in the midbody than a slow-speed boat, and may also be slightly beamier to increase lift. The midbody deadrise angle may be carried all the way to the transom for a softer ride, or it may flatten out slightly aft for better hydrodynamic lift.

STERN

The stern of a semiplaning boat is often a smaller version of the midbody section, though it may have slightly less deadrise. The buttock lines often run almost straight from the midbody to a transom stern that abruptly ends the hull.

Many semiplaning hulls carry a small skeg, although the majority have no keel or skeg at all. Without a skeg, the props are unprotected, making them vulnerable to damage in shallow water.

SUMMARY

Each of the three major hull forms is designed to meet unique requirements. The displacement hull is primarily a load-carrying hull. Semiplaning hulls operate just below planing conditions and tend to give a softer ride than higher speed hulls. A sportfishing hull has to get to the fishing grounds quickly, but then it will operate at trolling speeds or be at rest. While at rest it has to be relatively stable. The high-speed hull is designed simply for maximum speed through the water. Its only limitations are that the engines and crew must fit in the boat. These differing requirements give rise to a particular shape for each boat.

COMMON QUESTIONS

Many questions about hull shapes go back to the dawn of new boat styles. Here we answer the most common.

A ROUNDED OR CHINED HULL: WHICH IS BEST?

In terms of speed potential there is little difference between a chined and a rounded hull. In the displacement mode, both are locked into a wavelength slightly longer than the LWL. It is when both boats are running at semidisplacement speeds in a seaway that the differences become apparent.

Round-bilge or lobster-boat-style hulls have a rounded or soft-chine hull and tend to be better boats in waves at semiplaning speeds. This fact was recognized as far back as World War II, when the German navy built E-boats using a round hull shape, while the British and U.S. navies built patrol boats with chined hulls. In heavy seas the German boats rode better and were able to power faster than the Allied vessels. In flat water or low wave conditions, however, the chined hulls were faster and more maneuverable, although the ride was slightly harder. Since that time variable deadrise has somewhat softened the ride for chined hulls (by permitting a sharper deadrise back to the midsection, becoming shallower aft for bearing and stability), but round hull forms still offer a softer ride in heavy seas.

How does this apply to your situation? If you frequently operate in high seas or strong winds, you may enjoy a smoother ride in a round-bilge boat. If you are going to run in an enclosed bay in fairly flat water, a low deadrise chine hull will be fast, fuel efficient, and comfortable enough. Of course, if flat-out speed in a seaway is what you care about, this argument is moot: you'll want a deep-V hull.

How Fast Will It Go?

A boat's top speed depends on the fuel load, number of people onboard, weight of gear, sea conditions, and other variables. However, you don't really want to know a boat's top pedal-to-the-metal speed, because you put undue strain on the engine running it flat out. A better question to ask is how fast the boat cruises in your local sea state, and at what rpm. Also ask what the fuel consumption is. These figures give you a much better idea of a boat's practical performance.

How Many People Can I Get Aboard?

How many passengers you can carry depends on the U.S. Coast Guard–mandated capacity certificate of the boat. This can be found on a sign placed aboard the boat and is based on a coast guard formula.

What Range Can I Expect?

To figure out how far your powerboat can go before you need to refuel, you need to find out how much fuel the engine or engines use per hour. For example, if your boat's cruising speed is 7.5 knots, and the engine uses 3 gallons (33 L) of fuel per hour at cruise, and the boat's tanks hold 240 gallons (908 L) of fuel, the boat's range will be 80 hours

$$240 \div 3 = 80$$

or 600 miles

$$240 \div 3 \times 7.5 = 600$$

Fuel consumption increases with speed, of course. Consequently, you should make a graph of your fuel consumption at different speeds to ascertain the boat's range and ensure that you do not run out of fuel. With a few simple calculations, you can estimate safe distances between refueling stops. These preparations are essential for a successful powerboating trip.

4

TOOLS TO HELP EVALUATE BOATS

IF YOU ARE IN THE MARKET for a boat or just want to comparison shop, you can use a few computational tools to help make comparisons. Since these numbers are nondimensional, they can be applied to any size boat. A word of caution, however: don't let the spread between boat sizes get too large, or the comparisons will be distorted. Try to keep a maximum range of about 8 to 10 feet (2.4–3 m) between the smallest and the largest.

SPEED–LENGTH RATIO

The speed–length (S/L) ratio is derived from the Froude number as described in chapter 1. It is

$$\frac{\text{boatspeed in knots}}{\sqrt{\text{WL}}}$$

An S/L of less than 1.5 shows that the boat is in the displacement mode. Above 2.5 (and sometimes even higher) the boat is planing. Between 1.5 and 2.5, the boat is operating in a semidisplacement mode.

DISPLACEMENT–LENGTH RATIO

Calculate a boat's displacement–length ratio by dividing the boat's displacement in pounds by 2,240 to get long tons. Divide this figure by one one-hundredth of the waterline length (in feet) cubed. In other words, the ratio is

$$\frac{\text{displacement} \div 2240}{(\text{LWL} \div 100)^3}$$

If a boat weighs in at 8,500 pounds (3,856 kg) on a waterline of 31 feet (9.5 m), the displacement–length ratio equals

$$\frac{8{,}500 \div 2{,}240}{(31 \div 100)^3} = \frac{3.795}{0.03} = 126$$

In general, the higher the number, the heavier the boat for its length, and the slower it is. In a seaway a heavier boat is likely to handle waves better than a similar lighter boat. Planing hulls are in the 130 to 220 range, whereas trawler hulls are above 300. Semiplaning boats are typically between 225 and 300.

Length-to-Beam Ratio

The length-to-beam ratio gives an indication of how long a boat is relative to its beam and allows you to compare two boats of different size. For example, comparing a 50-foot (15.3 m) cruiser with a 12-foot (3.7 m) beam to a 40-foot (12.21 m) cruiser with a 10-foot (3 m) beam, we find that the larger boat has a length-to-beam ratio of 4.167, while the smaller boat has a ratio of 4. For its length, the smaller boat has more beam. A smaller ratio indicates a boat with greater transverse stability, making it better for trolling or drifting in beam seas.

Power-to-Weight Ratio

Some designers use the power-to-weight ratio to indicate whether a boat has sufficient horsepower for its weight. The ratio is engine horsepower divided by the displacement of the hull. Note that this is not a true nondimensional coefficient, but merely an indicator of the amount of horsepower a boat needs to push its weight through the water. When comparing boats, make sure that you use the same horsepower number, be it brake horsepower (bhp) or shaft horsepower (shp).

The ratio is

$$\frac{horsepower}{displacement}$$

Cubic Number

This is another good way to compare two boats of different size. By multiplying waterline length by the boat's beam and depth (from the bottom of the hull to the deck edge), you get the cubic number (CN).

For example, let's say one boat is 30 feet (9.14 m) on the waterline and has a maximum beam of 10 feet (3.04 m) and a depth of 6 feet (1.83 m), and therefore a CN of 1,800 cubic feet (50.9 cu. m). A second boat with a length of 34 feet (10.36 m), 11 feet (3.35 m) of beam, and a depth of 7 feet (2.13 m) has a CN of 2,618 feet (73.9 m). By dividing the CN of the first boat into the CN of the second boat, you can see that the second boat is 2,618 ÷ 1,800 = 1.45 (73.9 m ÷ 50.9 cu. m = 1.45) times as large as the first boat. In other words, it is 45 percent larger and, all other things being equal, should cost more to buy and maintain.

Note that some designers divide the CN by the volume of the boat's displacement to get an even more instructive number. This is done by taking the displacement in pounds (or kilograms) and dividing it by 64 (64 lb./29 kg of seawater in a cubic foot). CN in cubic feet divided by the displacement in pounds gives another number known as a *block coefficient* that is also handy for comparing boats.

Prismatic Coefficient

The prismatic coefficient is the ratio of the largest underwater section of the hull multiplied by the hull's waterline length, to the volume of displacement of the boat. In other words, you would need to find the volume of the half-tube (in the case of a round-bottom boat) or V-shaped wedge (in the case of a deep-V hull) whose cross section is the boat's largest underwater section and whose length is the boat's waterline, then divide that by the hull volume in cubic feet.

The optimum prismatic ratio varies in direct proportion to the hull resistance and the boat speed. Unfortunately, this means that it is impossible to design a boat with the optimum prismatic for all speeds. Designers use their experience and knowledge of other designs to select the best prismatic for the style and speed of boat they're designing. Variations in the prismatic coefficients of similar boats often can lead to big, seemingly inexplicable differences in performance.

The prismatic coefficient of a powerboat hull should become higher as boat speed increases—up to a certain limit. Obviously, the fastest boat is not a barge with a prismatic of 1. A typical displacement hull may have a prismatic coefficient of around 0.55 to 0.65, whereas a boat operating in the transitional zone may have a higher prismatic. A high-speed deep-V hull can have a prismatic coefficient as high as 0.75. Put another way, a planing hull needs to be fuller in the ends—especially aft—to develop dynamic lift.

5

POWERBOAT STYLING

WE'VE ALL SEEN THEM, those megayachts with oval windows, slanted stacks, wings, acres of wooden decks, and enough paint to cover Chicago three times. They are the far-out leading edge of the stylist's art—some would say far over the leading edge!

Most thinking boat designers ask themselves what these boats would be like in a bad storm. Would heavy seas cave in gigantic oval windows? Would the boat roll heavily with all that top hamper?

Aesthetics are part of yacht design and often can influence other parts of the design. For example, a large stack or funnel might make a boat look traditional or interesting, but it also puts a lot of extra weight high up and reduces stability. Most boats have only a small exhaust line from a diesel engine and use the stack space for storage instead. Nonetheless, a boat should be pleasing to the person who will buy and sail it. Styling is not an easy task, and its goal is often simply to set a yacht apart, but by following a few basic tenets most boats can be made to look attractive.

HULL STYLING

With careful design, each part of the boat contributes harmoniously to the whole. Good styling starts with the sheerline and progresses to the deck lines. The bow and the stern are almost incidental endings to the sheerline. Then there's freeboard: too much doesn't work on a short boat. In general, the longer the boat, the easier it is to incorporate high freeboard. Beyond these rules and a few others, styling becomes a matter of personal taste or the taste of the design and marketing departments of a production boat builder.

DEVELOPING THE SHEERLINE

Let's look at the process from the point of view of the designer. Starting with a blank sheet of paper, we draw the bow and stern on it and develop a sheerline. The straight line parallel to the waterline gives us a reference point for the sheerline. In general, the lowest point on the sheer is at station 7 or 8, with the sheerline at station 10

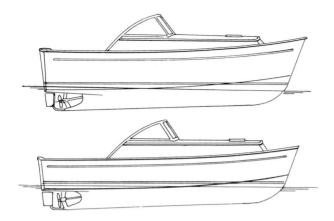

High freeboard tends to look ugly on a small boat. In the top sketch the freeboard is high and the cabintop low, resulting in a chunky-looking boat. In the lower drawing the freeboard has been lowered and the cabintop raised to give a more attractive look.

about half the height of station 0. If we decide that the boat needs more spring to the sheer, we can easily adjust it while keeping the same proportions.

As a point of interest, the sheerlines of wooden boats were traditionally developed *in situ* (in place on the hull) by bolting a sheer plank at the bow and allowing it to assume its natural bend down the side of the hull. Because the sides of a hull slope outward at the bow, the plank naturally kicked lower as the hull became wider. As the hull narrowed up again and

the planking became more vertical toward the stern the plank rose up slightly, creating the classic sheerline. Even though the widest part of a hull is usually between stations 6 and 7, most designers now put the low point of the sheerline nearer station 8 to get the right look to the hull profile. This rule is not rigid, of course, but provides a general guide for setting a traditional sheerline on a boat.

A high-speed powerboat has very different requirements, because it tends to trim up by the bow when accelerating onto a

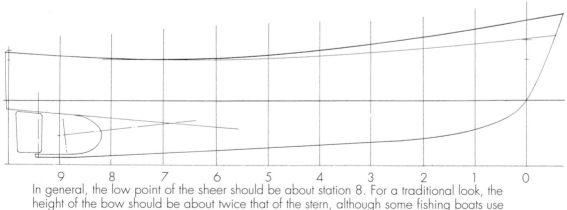

In general, the low point of the sheer should be about station 8. For a traditional look, the height of the bow should be about twice that of the stern, although some fishing boats use a factor of three or more.

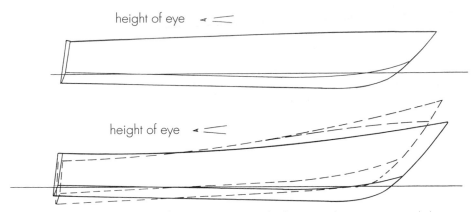

height of eye

height of eye

As a high-speed boat starts onto a plane, it trims up at the bow. With a conventional sheer line the view over the bow becomes obstructed and at a critical moment the person at the helm cannot see anything in front of the boat. Lowering the sheerline forward makes it easier for the helmsman to see and much safer.

plane. With the helmsman well aft on a boat with a conventional sheerline, it becomes extremely difficult to see forward. Consequently, the sheerline of a high-speed boat is lowered forward to improve visibility. On very modern boats many designers use an absolutely flat sheerline, but in my opinion this only works well if the boat is indeed ultramodern. On other styles, flat sheer doesn't work so well.

Special Sheerline Problems

Some sheerlines must be high by necessity. An example is the small cruiser where the marketing goal is to have full headroom inside the boat. From the designer's standpoint, this is best solved by adding long horizontal lines to disguise the height. In one approach, a false sheerline is shown lower on the hull and the deck line raised. Interior standing headroom is achieved, but the sheerline looks lower. The lines of a rubrail or a wide boottop can also help disguise freeboard height.

Another common sheerline problem is the discontinuous sheer, since breaking a line as strong as the sheerline automatically makes a boat appear taller. Rather than breaking the sheerline, it can be run forward and a second sheerline worked in above the first. The resultant long horizontal stripes help to disguise high freeboard. In general, horizontal lines lengthen the look of a boat, whereas vertical lines shorten it and make it appear taller.

DEVELOPING THE BOW AND STERN

Early in the design process the bow and the stern are straight lines. Now we'll play with their curves to get them right. For a trawler-style yacht with a lot of spring to the sheerline, we might want to make the bow straight, whereas on a tug yacht we might make the bow more vertical or give it a little reverse knuckle. This styling was used in powerboats around 1900 and appears to be making a comeback today on faster, high-speed hulls. If the boat is to have an older, Edwardian-era styling, then we might use a clipper bow, which works well with a short bowsprit or anchor handling platform.

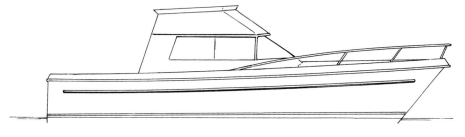

More modern boats may have a straight sheerline, but the end result is a boxy-looking boat.

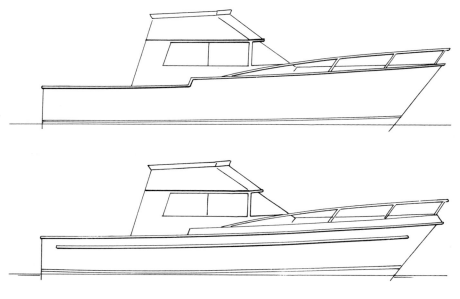

A broken sheerline tends to make a boat look taller *(top)*, whereas carrying the lower part of the sheerline forward and dropping in a false sheer above it *(bottom)* makes the boat look longer and more attractive.

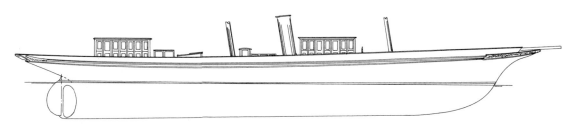

The long rubrail and sheer strake make this old-style boat look very long indeed. The clipper bow with its bowsprit and long stern overhang further help to elongate the bow and create a sense of great elegance.

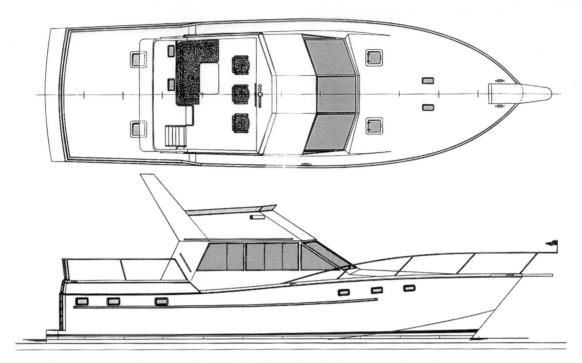

Bow shape matters. In this cruiser designed by the author the bow is straight, in keeping with the angular look of the superstructure.

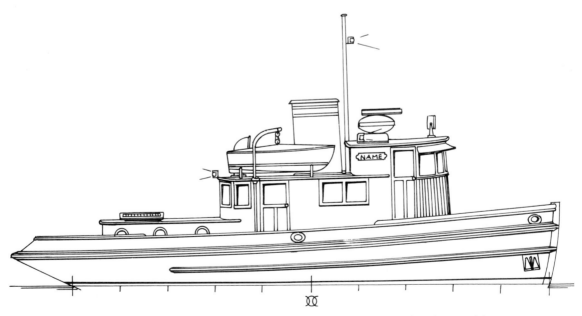

A plumb bow suits the look of this 1920s-style, 44-foot-long (13.4 m) tug, also designed by the author.

The stern should be matched to the bow profile. A stubby trawler yacht might have a vertical transom or one with a step. Because it is a slow displacement hull, the tug yacht might have a rounded stern. A traditionally styled picnic launch might have a fantail stern similar in shape to the tug stern, or even a reverse stern, slightly longer than on a fast boat to reflect the finer lines of a displacement hull.

These bow and stern shapes can be fitted to the same sheerline to make boats of very different styling. If we vary the sheer somewhat, we can make the hulls even more suited to their purpose.

ADDING THE SUPERSTRUCTURE

Now we need to add a superstructure that reflects the style most suited to the boat. For example, a trawler yacht style may want cabin space forward, a bridge, and a saloon aft. By putting a small stack abaft the bridge and a stub mast, we get a look that is perfectly traditional for a trawler yacht. We can add the same features using a much more modern styling to get an updated version of the same boat, or by changing styles yet again we can make the boat look really old-time and more like a tug yacht. All these changes are made on the same sheerline and hull lines and do not at all affect interior space.

Styling the superstructure is largely a matter of personal whim or designing to the client's needs, but there are a number of factors that make the structure more homogeneous. All the major lines are taken to a single point located somewhere above the drawing. This has the effect of integrating the entire profile.

Lines from structural supports, windows, and doors also can be used to enhance a look of total integration. These lines may all be upright, or they may be sloped slightly to suit the look of the upperworks. Although this is slightly more expensive to produce, it strengthens the integrated look of the structure.

On some boats the cabintop can be used to strengthen the sheerline. It might, for example, have a reverse slope that emulates

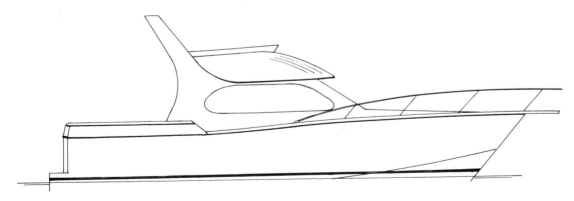

Although the style of the hull can certainly influence a boat's looks, it is the superstructure that most people look at. This is the same hull as opposite, top, but with a radically different superstructure, making the boat look very different.

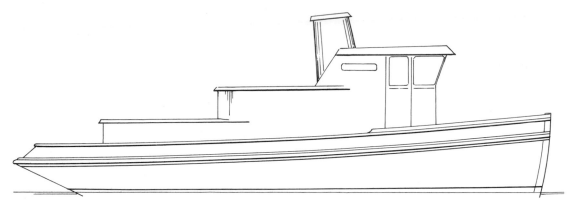

We can make the tug in the drawing on the bottom of page 53 look much more modern using the same hull but a different superstructure, as shown here.

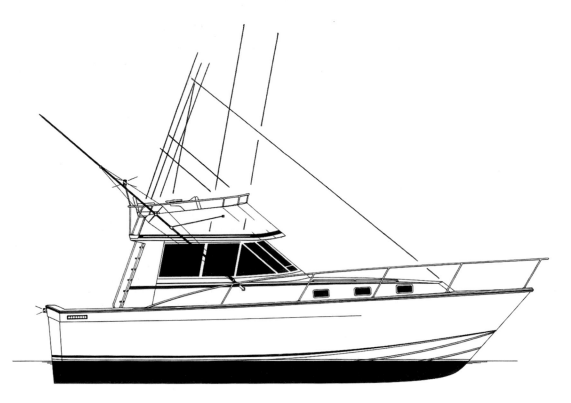

Good styling often means that all the major lines are drawn in the same plane to help integrate the profile. In fact, the windows in this design are not quite held in the same plane, and if you look at the drawing carefully they look slightly askew. When working with a large drawing on the drafting table or a computer screen, a slight error like this is difficult to spot. In the old-time drawing offices, some designers used to put a drawing on the floor and stand on a chair for a distant view to make sure it looked properly integrated.

the sheerline and helps to make the boat look longer than it really is. Keeping the tops and bottoms of windows in the same plane further enhances the effect.

AVOIDING CLUTTER

With the basic design worked out, it is time to add the deck gear and other equipment that is needed on a boat. Lifelines, stanchions, bow rails, cleats, anchor windlass, hawsepipes, anchors, and other gear all complicate the look of a design, but they are essential equipment and part of the overall look of the boat. To help reduce the clutter, many boatbuilders resort to a hiding strategy: they use pop-up cleats, or deck openings with recessed cleats, to maintain a sleek and stylish look. The anchor, for example, can be fitted on a bow roller ready for use, with the chain led aft to a windlass recessed into a bow locker.

This look can be dangerous, however, if there are no handholds for crew walking on the foredeck. There must be a way for a crewman to get to the bow without losing contact with the boat. Forcing a crew to negotiate a wide expanse of foredeck before grabbing the bow rail is dangerous, despite the fact that it is fairly commonplace. When adding or hiding clutter, think about how the crew move around on the boat and make sure they are safe. Crew safety is of greater importance than a sleekly styled boat (for more information on deck safety, see chapter 8).

Anchor Handling Gear

An anchor handling platform is often added to a boat as an afterthought after has been built . . . and it looks that way. Bolted

This Henriquez has a substantial bow rail to keep crew aboard as they move toward the bow. This photo is taken from the bow, looking aft.

to the deck, it intrudes on the slight, fair curve of the deck crown profile. Adding an anchor handling platform when the boat is being designed is quite easy, and the results are more satisfying; with a few minor changes its styling can be integrated into the overall design. In one approach, the deck camber at the bow is lowered to make the anchor-handling platform a fair extension of the sheerline. Not only does this make the platform look like part of the boat, it also makes the boat look longer and lower.

Radar Arches

One of the most difficult problems on a boat is to add a radar arch or T-top without ruining the line of the hull. There are several feasible solutions. Sloping the structure to mimic the forward part of the boat carries the eye away from the hull, giving the impression of speed. Sloping the radar arch aft impart grace, while sloping it forward gives a slight impression of huskiness or power—a more aggressive character, perhaps. The greater the slope, the more these features are emphasized. Unless the boat is a traditional design, the radar arch should never stand upright.

Stacks

Exhaust stacks are not for everyone or every boat. They go best with more traditional designs. A big stack on an old-style tug replica, for example, has lots of style and can be used for fender and dock line stowage. On a more modern-looking power yacht, a lower and smaller stack helps bring the eye to the middle of the boat, providing a focal point.

Aesthetic appeal is personal and subjective. Decide what you consider stylish and go ahead with it. Your boat will be more satisfying to own and use if it is an expression of your taste.

A bolt-on anchor handling platform looks like an add-on *(top)*. The integrated anchor platform on the Wellcraft 270 Coastal *(bottom)* tends to lengthen the boat and make it more attractive. *(Bottom: Wellcraft Marine)*

6

UNDERSTANDING STABILITY

WHEN YOU WALK FROM one side of an anchored boat to the other, you instinctively feel whether it tips too far or too readily. Similarly, when you're on a moving boat going into a turn, you sense how far it heels. If the boat heels too far, you might wonder about its stability. But stability is rarely uppermost in our minds when we evaluate a boat; factors such as speed, comfort, and amenities often have a greater influence on our senses. We are inclined to assume that the stability is adequate; after all, stability is not a criterion that you can measure without some effort. (The calculations are simple once you understand them. Performing a heeling test, however, takes time, and calculating the weights by hand takes forever.)

In fact, very few new boats ever reach a buyer without having adequate stability, but a boatowner can thereafter affect the stability quite easily. Let us say, for example, that a fish is sighted and everyone rushes to one side of the boat to get a glimpse. The boat heels dramatically to that side, but assuming it's not dangerously overloaded to begin with, its stability will still be adequate and it will stay upright.

It is a different matter when you bring a large fish aboard a small boat. Suppose you try to bring a giant tuna aboard a 26-foot (7.9 m) sportfishing boat. If the tuna weighs about 850 pounds (385 kg, or the equivalent to four or five people) and your transom door is to port, you have added 850 pounds of load to one side of the boat. Now you have 40 miles (64 km) to get home and the boat has a definite list to port. How dangerous is the additional heel? Should you head for home and hope for the best? Cut up the fish and redistribute its weight? Or dump it overboard in the interest of safety?

Other factors must enter the equation. The weight of the fish has reduced the freeboard and made the boat more liable to flooding. (There have been cases where a big load of fish has put the scuppers underwater and flooded the boat. This also means that hatches in the cockpit should be watertight.) To understand the effects of these factors on stability, it helps to look at the variables the way a designer does.

The designer must ensure adequate stability along two axes: the *transverse* axis (i.e., side to side) and the *longitudinal* (fore-and-aft) direction. Stability also can be *passive* or *dynamic*. In most cases it is measured in the passive, or static, condition (i.e., with the boat at rest), simply because calculations of stability for a boat underway are complex and difficult, though some of the latest computer programs give good estimates. If the passive stability is adequate, the dynamic condition (with the boat underway) is often assumed to be adequate. Rough sea conditions, high-speed running, heavy loads of people or cargo, flooding from boarding seas or leaks, and sharp turns all can affect a boat's dynamic stability, but in general, designers' assumptions are safe and boats have adequate stability. (We can calculate the effect of overloading the boat and predict what happens when the boat is flooded using passive stability techniques.)

On monohulls, transverse stability—the measure of a boat's resistance to heeling from side to side—is generally lower than longitudinal stability. Thus, a lack of transverse stability causes most monohull capsizes. Things are different aboard a multihull, where transverse stability may be almost as high as longitudinal stability.

FACTORS AFFECTING TRANSVERSE STABILITY

The two major factors that affect transverse stability are, first, the shape of the waterplane (the "footprint" of the boat seen from above if it were sliced from bow to stern at the waterline; see chapter 2) and, second, the boat's centers of gravity and buoyancy. The waterplane shape determines what is known as *form stability*. The height of the vertical center of buoyancy (VCB), which is the centroid of the hull volume, and the height of the vertical center of gravity (VCG) determine what we'll call *weight stability* to distinguish it from form stability. VCG is in turn determined by the distribution of major weights (engines, tanks, auxiliary generators, ballast, etc.) in the hull and will change if you add, subtract, or move around heavy objects. Both locations (VCB and VCG) can be said to revolve around a virtual center known as the *metacenter* (M). The relationship among these three centers determines how much—or how little—weight stability a boat has. (Similarly, the LCG, LCB, and longitudinal metacenter have a relationship that covers longitudinal stability, as discussed in chapter 3.)

FORM STABILITY

The wider or beamier a boat—where the vertical centers of buoyancy and gravity stay constant—the harder it is to tip over. Just as a pyramid standing on its wide, flat base is hard to turn over, and a car with a wider wheelbase gives a more stable ride, a wide-based boat such as a catamaran or trihedral hull form (like the Boston Whaler) provides high form stability. In contrast, a narrow boat, such as a canoe, will turn over easily.

When a person climbs into a canoe, its center of gravity rises, and with little form stability, it may easily capsize. The canoeist counteracts the capsize tendency by moving his or her body weight—that is, center of gravity—as far down in the boat as possible. We can increase the canoe's form

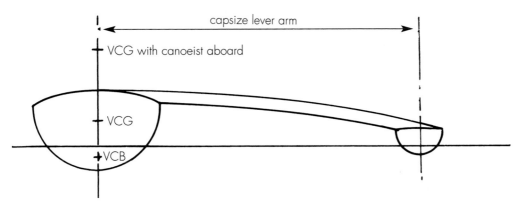

A narrow-hulled vessel such as a canoe does not have a lot of vertical stability. The canoeist climbing aboard *(top)* raises the vertical center of gravity (VCG), thereby making the canoe vulnerable to capsizing. The VCB is the centroid of the immersed hull volume and does not change. However, when a canoeist climbs aboard, the hull sinks in the water slightly and the VCB rises slightly. The difference between VCG and VCB controls the stability of the vessel. An outrigger *(bottom)* increases form stability and makes the canoe more resistant to capsizing.

stability by fitting it with an outrigger, but this added resistance to capsize comes at the price of additional weight and resistance.

On a larger powerboat, the waterplane shape is the unchangeable part of the stability equation. Compare the waterplane shapes shown in the accompanying drawing. The first is a long, narrow, canoelike hull. The second is a round-stern hull. The third is a sportfisherman (transom-stern powerboat), and the fourth is a catamaran-

style hull. The canoe-style hull has a length-to-beam ratio of over 7, while the round-stern boat has a ratio of 3.4. The transom-stern sportfisherman comes in at about 2.8, and the catamaran at 1.8. Assuming an equivalent center of gravity and similar hull lengths, the resistance to capsize of these hulls varies inversely with their length-to-beam ratios. Also keep in mind that a longer boat of the same shape as a smaller vessel will have more stability simply because of its increased size.

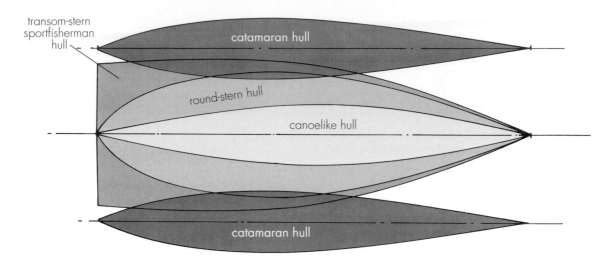

Superimposed waterplane views for several powerboats of the same length. If the CG and CB were the same for each boat, the boat with the canoelike waterplane would capsize first, the round-stern boat next, the transom-stern sportfisherman third, and finally the catamaran. In other words, the catamaran hull has the greatest form stability.

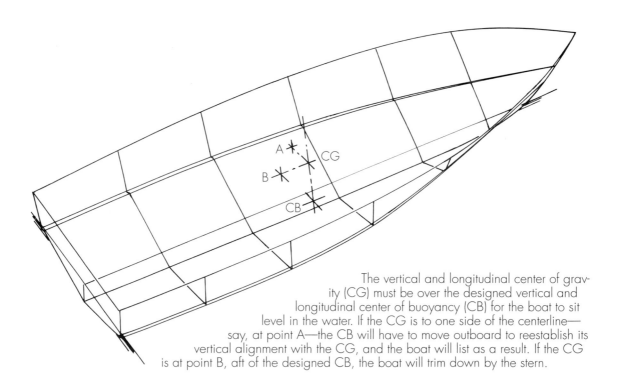

The vertical and longitudinal center of gravity (CG) must be over the designed vertical and longitudinal center of buoyancy (CB) for the boat to sit level in the water. If the CG is to one side of the centerline—say, at point A—the CB will have to move outboard to reestablish its vertical alignment with the CG, and the boat will list as a result. If the CG is at point B, aft of the designed CB, the boat will trim down by the stern.

CENTER OF GRAVITY

The center of gravity (CG) is the point at which the entire weight of the boat is said to act in order to make the calculation easier. To find it, a designer must calculate the vertical and longitudinal centers of gravity of every item on the boat in its normal location, and then find their combined centers using vector addition. For the boat to trim level, the LCG must lie directly over the designed center of buoyancy (LCB). When the owner starts moving, adding, or subtracting weights (people, fuel oil, water, stores, dinghies, gear, etc.), the CG will change in ways the designer may not have anticipated, and the CB will shift to meet it. When a new equilibrium is established, the boat may no longer be in level trim.

In a typical powerboat, the vertical component or height of the center of gravity (VCG) is usually near or just above the waterline. Designers want it as low as possible, so they place heavy weights such as tanks and engines well down in the hull. The longitudinal center of gravity (LCG) is typically around 52 to 64 percent of the waterline aft of the bow, though it may be farther aft on a high-speed powerboat due to the large volume of hull aft. The CG must be on the transverse centerline, of course, or the boat will list to one side.

Lowering the VCG is probably the easiest method of improving a boat's transverse stability. On a powerboat, an owner can fill fuel or water tanks, but it is difficult to do much more than that unless you are prepared to fit heavier engines or to lighten the topsides by removing heavy gear. Adverse changes to the VCG can be extremely dangerous. For example, suppose you want to make a long trip and place several 55-gallon (208 L) drums of fuel oil on the foredeck. Their weight not only submerges the bow and lifts the stern out of the water, thus changing the shape of the boat's waterplane (often making it narrower), it also raises the VCG. The combined effect could be enough to render the boat unstable, especially in heavy seas. Alternatively, imagine an entire crew gathering on a flybridge. Eight people weighing about 160 pounds (72 kg) each would move 1,280 pounds (580 kg) about 6 feet (1.8 m) upward, substantially raising the VCG.

When a number of people go from one side of the boat to the other or up to the flybridge, they don't change the weight of the boat, but they have a pronounced impact on the boat's transverse and vertical CG. Moving to one side causes the boat to heel, which in turn, changes the shape of the waterplane. On a boat with vertical sides it actually might reduce the waterplane area, which further increases the heeling. The farther outboard the people go, the more the boat will heel.

The sidebar on page 65 shows the various points a naval architect uses to calculate stability. (Note: Naval architecture convention shows the waterline, rather than the vessel, heeled.) A truer measure of tenderness or stiffness is the time taken for a vessel to roll from one side to the other, but this is more difficult to calculate, so a stability calculation as shown here is made instead. The result is commonly called *righting moment* but is, in fact, *restoring moment*, or the moment required to restore the boat to its upright condition. A *low righting moment* means a tender boat, while a *high righting moment* makes for a stiff boat. A tender boat heels quickly in response to wind and wave, whereas a stiff boat resists heeling with a jerky, wearing motion. Too much of either is bad for a boat and its crew.

CHINES AND CHINE FLATS

Chines and associated chine flats that curve up out of the water forward bring reserve transverse stability into play when the boat loaded. When three or four people and their attendant gear and supplies board a boat, it settles on its waterline and more of the chine length is immersed, thus increasing stability.

LONGITUDINAL STABILITY

All the factors that affect transverse stability also apply to longitudinal stability, but more so. Because a boat is typically about three times as long as it is wide, longitudinal stability is much higher than transverse stability. This means that tipping a boat down by the bow is harder than heeling it, and flipping it end over end is very difficult indeed (though it has been known to occur).

Interestingly, ultra-high-speed boats such as *Miss Budweiser*, an unlimited hydroplane (see photo in chapter 1), are about twice as wide as they are long and can flip end over end when racing. These boats have a trihedral underbody configuration with wide sponsons forward and a single planing surface aft, and they run at speeds near 200 mph (322 kph).

TENDER AND STIFF BOATS

It may seem logical that increasing stability is good, but too much stability, like too much of most things, is bad. A boat with high stability will heel when the heeling force (wind or sea state) is large enough, but the boat will try to return to the upright position as quickly as possible. The vessel's motion will be jerky as it tries to stay in the vertical position. In extreme cases, this motion can be violent enough to injure crew. The only cure is to raise the boat's VCG until the motion is easier, which might mean fitting a tower, adding heavy chairs or gear aloft, or even, as has been done in extreme cases, bolting lead ingots to the deckhead.

On the other hand, tender boats tend to roll and stay heeled for long periods of time, which can be quite frightening and is undesirable. Such a tendency should be corrected by adding lead ballast to the bilge or removing heavy items from high positions in the boat.

STABILITY AT LARGE ANGLES OF HEEL

A boat can have stability at all angles of heel until a point of vanishing stability is found, as shown in the *righting moment curve* on page 66. The point of vanishing stability is at a very high angle of heel, usually over 100 degrees and usually after the edge of the deck has been immersed. The curve shows, however, that righting moment begins to decrease well before it vanishes altogether. This means that the righting moment is actually smaller at large

How Stability Is Calculated

Stability is calculated by first finding the center of buoyancy (CB), which is also the center of volume of the immersed part of the hull. This position is found from a hydrostatic calculation and is often designated graphically as point B. The vertical center of gravity (VCG) is then found from a vector sum of component weights and can be designated as G. The center of gravity will lie directly above the center of buoyancy as long as the boat is in level trim. WL is the waterline when the boat is upright, and $W_1 L_1$ is the waterline when the boat is heeled. The heel angle is emphasized for clarity.

The next step is to heel the boat. Usually designers heel the boat 1 degree because the first 15 to 20 degrees of the stability curve is relatively straight, and 1 degree provides a reference point to compare against other designs. When the boat is heeled 1 degree, point B moves to new position B_1. A line projected vertically through B_1 crosses the extended centerline of the vessel at point M. The height of M above the VCG, or point G, is known as the *metacentric height* (GM), and M is often said to be the *metacenter*. The horizontal distance or arm GZ is known as the *righting lever*. GZ multiplied by the displacement of the vessel gives the righting moment in foot-pounds.

By lowering the ballast, a designer can lower point G, which makes GZ longer and increases stability. If the beam is increased, B_1 will shift farther from B with each angle of heel (at least initially), which again makes GZ longer.

Note that in the days before computers, a boat was occasionally designed with the position M below the position G. A boat with negative GM will tend to heel over and stay heeled over—a very undesirable situation, akin to having a pyramid balanced on its head waiting for some force to topple it over.

Note also that stability can be transverse or longitudinal. When stability is measured longitudinally, the letters remain the same but the numbers usually get much higher.

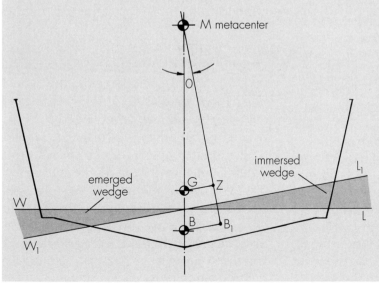

How a naval architect calculates stability. B is the center of buoyancy, or the center of volume of the immersed portion of the hull. G is the center of gravity of the boat. GM is the metacentric height of the boat, which is more or less constant over low angles of heel. For the boat to be stable, G must be below M. As the boat heels, B moves to point B_1. The moment to right the boat is found from GZ times the displacement. Naval architects call this moment a *restoring moment*, whereas most boaters use the term *righting moment*.

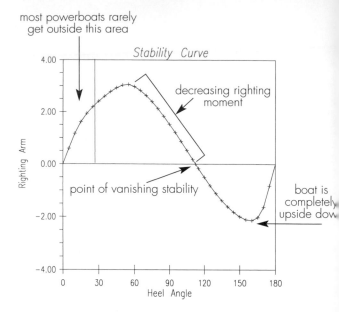

most powerboats rarely get outside this area

Stability Curve

decreasing righting moment

point of vanishing stability

boat is completely upside down

Righting Arm

Heel Angle

The stability or righting moment curve for a typical powerboat as developed using the Prosurf system from New Wave Systems. Notice how the curve increases in a straight line to about 20 degrees. In practice, few powerboats heel much more than this. The stability of this powerboat reaches its peak at around 60 degrees and turns negative at around 115 degrees. When the curve turns downward the boat's resistance to capsize begins to decrease, and when it turns negative, the boat will continue to roll over without further outside influence.

angles of heel. To state it differently, once the boat graphed here is pushed over to 60 degrees in a big sea, its resistance to further heeling will lessen. It still wants to right itself, but not as forcefully.

For this reason, and because water has usually found its way below by the time a boat is heeled to about 70 degrees (a factor not considered in the righting moment curve), designers assume 70 degrees as a practical maximum permissible heel. In other words, if wind, sea, or loading conditions heel a boat past 70 degrees, it is likely to capsize because the righting moment trying to restore it to the upright condition decreases.

In practice, a recreational powerboat rarely heels beyond 20 to 25 degrees, so a boatowner need not worry much about heeling to an excessive angle. It is a scenario more likely to be experienced by a commercial fishing boat in winter with ice on its upper works, or a boat with a load of fish or a cargo that has shifted. The rest of us can take comfort from the old saw: "Your boat can take more than you can."

EFFECTS OF FLOODING ON STABILITY

If you have ever inadvertently flooded the cockpit while backing down or tried to move around in a swamped dinghy, you will have experienced firsthand the effect of free surface. *Free surface* refers to uncontained liquid inside a container (in this case, a boat), which effect is to exaggerate pitching and rolling, thus increasing the vessel's tendency to capsize. When a boat with a flooded cockpit heels, the water moves to the low side of the cockpit, increasing the weight on that side of the boat, which in turn increases the heeling angle. It also moves the center of gravity of the liquid. This movement can be said to act through a virtual metacenter (M_1). The designer treats this situation as a rise in the CG (G in drawing), which reduces the metacentric height (GM, but M in drawing) and the righting lever (GZ), and ultimately reduces the righting moment of the vessel.

When liquid is contained in a full tank,

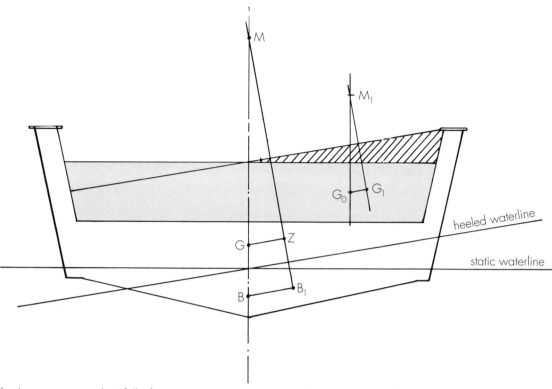

If a boat gets a cockpit full of water or is swamped, its stability is reduced. This is because the center of gravity of the uncontained water lurches in the direction of heel, exaggerating the heel in a self-reinforcing feedback loop. This is the **free-surface effect**. Here, for simplicity, we call the CB simply B, and the CG just G.

the surface of the liquid cannot move and the tank is considered as a solid unit whose CG is at the center of volume. If the tank is only half full, however, the liquid can move and the position of its CG therefore changes. Although this effect is negligible for boats with small tanks, it can be significant for a boat with very large fuel or water tanks.

Free surface, in general, destabilizes a boat and should be avoided if at all possible. A filled cockpit should be drained as quickly as possible, and at such times it also helps to move people down from a flybridge or other high point, where they raise the CG and hence further destabilize the boat.

7

SEAWORTHINESS

WHAT IS SEAWORTHINESS? Is it conferred by the shape of a hull, or by its strength? Is it the skipper's ability to handle the boat? Or is it carrying enough equipment to be prepared for every emergency? Is it knowing how to prepare for heavy weather, or how to navigate in poor visibility?

Seaworthiness is all of these and more. It is foremost a highly subjective term. Seaworthiness is hard to evaluate because it is comprised of many things and can change from one boat or crew to the next. It is also defined to a large extent by the bias of the person rendering the judgment. For example, a surveyor I know will not declare any boat seaworthy, because his experience says that seaworthiness is totally determined by the vessel operator and that the surveyor is not in a position to assess a skipper's ability. To some extent he is right, although other factors are obviously involved.

The conditions in which a boat is to be used help to determine the features required of a seaworthy boat. For an offshore power cruiser, it certainly helps to have watertight interior bulkheads, a watertight engine compartment, and a small cockpit. But these features may be detrimental on a boat intended for puttering around Narragansett or Tampa Bay because they add weight and complexity and make the boat difficult to operate.

THE SKILL OF THE SKIPPER AND CREW

Exactly how does the skill of the skipper and crew affect a boat's seaworthiness? The connection comes in knowing how to handle a boat in adverse conditions. Skilled boaters know to slow down when powering into a strong wind and heavy sea. They know that waves are steeper in the early part of the storm and so will power the boat more slowly as the storm sets in, but as the storm increases in strength and waves increase in length, skilled skippers might increase speed slightly.

Skilled skippers also check the weather report before heading to sea. Passage of a cold front might change the wind from a warm southerly to a cold and gusty northeasterly, in a matter of hours. The front itself might be accompanied by rain, hail, high winds, thunder, and lightning.

Savvy skippers might haul their boats and put them ashore before bad weather hits. To help ease wind pressure on the hull and mooring, they might strip off T-tops and awnings before high winds arrive. All these judgments are a part of being a seaworthy boater.

A SEAWORTHY HULL

A seaworthy hull will have adequate stability and a smooth motion in a seaway. A boat with a jerky motion will fatigue its crew, and tired crews make bad decisions. A seaworthy hull also will have adequate buoyancy forward and enough freeboard throughout to help keep water off the deck.

It should be well engineered, though not necessarily heavy. Heavy displacement does not automatically confer seaworthiness. Adequate displacement is certainly a factor in reducing motion and minimizing crew fatigue, but a badly engineered heavy boat is less seaworthy than a well-engineered light one.

The shape of the hull is certainly a factor. Increasing the deadrise angle in a V-bottom boat is one way to make it more suitable for heavy seas. Lower deadrise produces higher slamming loads on the flat bottom than do higher deadrise angles, which means that the hull bottom panels must be sufficiently strong or they will deflect inward, ultimately leading to failure. Typically, structural features such as longitudinal stringers, which also may form the engine beds, run from near the bow to the transom in order to reinforce the bottom panels.

On a slower boat, a long keel or a skeg often adds appreciably to a vessel's strength and seaworthiness. Because of their lateral resistance, keels and skegs help to resist yawing (turning from side to side) and rolling in a seaway. Bilge keels on a round-bottomed displacement hull also minimize yawing and rolling without increasing draft.

SEAWORTHINESS BELOWDECKS

Seaworthy interiors are increasingly rare on production cruising boats. Very few boats are built with seaworthy bunks, even fewer are built with sufficient handholds, and rarer yet is the boat with unvarnished cabin sole boards. A seaworthy bunk is one in which the occupant can stay reasonably secure and comfortable even in the worst conditions. This means it should be just wide and long enough and should run fore and aft with the head end forward so that you don't sleep with your head down when the boat trims up by the bow. The bunk should have plenty of headroom and be equipped with a securely fastened lee cloth.

Although most cruising boats have bunks in the bow, these become virtually uninhabitable when a boat is banging into a head sea. If you need to sleep when large seas are running, you may be better off pulling a mattress onto the cabin sole near the middle of the boat than trying to sleep in a bouncy forward V-berth.

Ideally, a bunk should run fore and aft, rather than transversely across the hull. A bunk at an angle across the hull will be hard to sleep in when the boat is rolling and banging into a head sea. In my opinion, the toilet unit should also be aligned fore and aft: that way, it's easier to brace yourself. If it is placed at an angle to the centerline, it might be difficult to wedge yourself into place.

On a seaworthy boat handholds are everywhere in the cabin. They should be on the corners of furniture, on the overhead, on ladders, and even on doors. There should be adequate rails around the stove. The galley sole should be nonskid, with knives securely fastened (not left loose in a knife rack where they can fly out and impale someone). Securely fastened drawers and sole boards fastened but not screwed down are other hallmarks of a seaworthy interior.

ENGINE ROOM

Seaworthiness extends to the engine compartment as well. The boat's battery bank should be firmly fastened in place, as should all toolboxes and stores such as cans of lubricating oil. The engine mounts should be suitable for the size of the engine and firmly mounted on strongly fabricated engine bearers. Doors to the engine compartment should be securely fastened (and watertight on offshore boats).

I was once on a powerboat that started to disintegrate as we pounded into a head sea. The experience is not one I care to repeat. On the bridge the engine roar covered noises from below, but at deck level we heard a deafening crash from the engine compartment. We hurriedly took up the engine compartment boards and peered below. A 40-gallon (150 L) can of lubricating oil was emptying into the bilge, where tools lay strewn about. By quick action we saved about half of the oil, but the tools were everywhere, many already in the sludge of the engine bilge. Before going to sea, secure all tools and tool boxes, oil, and other loose gear.

Anything that can come loose should be considered potentially dangerous. This means that batteries, battery trays, air cylinders, propane tanks, spare parts, gratings, and ladders should be bolted or locked down before dock lines are cast off. Only in this way can you stop disasters from happening.

Carry spare parts such as fuel filters, belts, lubricating oil, and even gasket kits, and know how to use them. Be prepared. It is the mark of a prudent boater.

SEAWORTHINESS ON DECK

Handholds, rails, and lifelines are essential to keeping crew safe and onboard. Handrails and protected access to the tower and foredeck are major considerations.

Seaworthiness starts at the helm station. Is visibility clear forward and to the sides? Can the person at the helm see the deck crew at all times? Can the cockpit drain quickly? Cockpit scuppers that drain over the side or transom are effective unless the boat is so heavily loaded that the scuppers sink under the water. Self-draining cockpits should be mandatory for all boats. If your boat has large scuppers, make sure you do not overload the boat and put them underwater. If there is any possibility that water might flood the cockpit, the hatches in the cockpit sole should be watertight.

Seaworthiness also means having strongly made, leakproof hatches on deck that open facing aft. Opening hatches that face forward tend to scoop water into the boat rather than shedding it. On a cruiser, a windshield for bad weather and a T-top for sunny weather are seamanlike.

When moving around on deck, check the handholds. There should be plenty of them, preferably inboard. Wherever you are on the boat you should be able to grasp a handhold, especially on the side- and foredecks. Ladders should have safety rails, and hatches between decks should have rails around them. On stepping off the bridge of one boat I know, you have to step around the hatch to the deck below. If you aren't paying attention, you step directly down the hatch. For this reason it is kept closed except to pass through. In my opinion, an access hatch at the top of a 10-foot (3 m) ladder that must remain closed is not a seaworthy feature.

To a large extent, seaworthiness is a state of mind. It involves an awareness of the value of preparing everything beforehand. It involves taking adequate precautions to ensure that your boat will return home uneventfully and that every contingency has been considered before you head for the open sea.

COMFORT

COMFORT ABOARD a boat takes many forms. There's the comfort of knowing your boat can handle everything the weather can throw at it. There's the comfort of knowing that the hull is strong enough to pound into big seas and get you home safely (see chapter 12, How a Boat Is Built). There is the comfort of knowing your boat is properly maintained. Then there are creature comforts. Air-conditioning on a very hot day . . . a nice seat in which to relax with a cool drink . . . a warm shower after you have been swimming in 60-degree (15°C) seawater. Comfort is all these things and more.

Some types of comfort should be designed into a boat. First and foremost is ride—harsh or soft? Second come seats and walkways, with other features crowding just behind. Access to both sides of twin engines may not seem like a comfort feature, but if the fuel oil filter is on the outboard side of an engine and you cannot reach it without lying on top of it, you may never change the filter. A clogged filter can significantly reduce your comfort level!

Other features can be added later. A T-top, for instance, may not be part of the boat when you purchase it, but it provides shade from the hot summer sun and is easily installed.

A COMFORTABLE HULL SHAPE

Speed and comfort are not compatible. In most seas, high-speed boats tend to fly into the air and slam down hard. A deep-V hull can mitigate the discomfort but can never eliminate it. On the other hand, slowing down increases comfort as does no other factor: if you want a comfortable ride, you need to slow down. That is one of the reasons most people cruise at slower speeds: the ride is easier and more comfortable. Plus, fuel consumption is better.

As explained in chapter 2, a warped-bottom or variable-deadrise hull tends to be more comfortable than a constant-deadrise hull, mostly because the underwater sections are somewhat finer forward, and this fineness is carried well aft, often to midships or even farther. The variable-deadrise hull is less likely to slam or pound, making the ride more enjoyable.

Boats with rounded hull shapes also tend to be more comfortable than flat-bottomed boats in a seaway. The rounded hull pounds less and gives an easier ride. If we were to combine all these comfort factors, we would find that a slower boat with a rounded bottom, small centerline keel for directional stability, and moderate beam would be more comfortable than a low-deadrise, hard-chine, high-speed boat. This is exactly the position the British motorized torpedo boat (MTB) operators found themselves in during World War II when the German round-bottomed E-boats proved more seaworthy in the short, steep seas of the English Channel and the North Sea. In flat water the British boats were both faster and had a better motion through the water. But when the seas got up, the German boats had a softer ride. The crossover point was about 30 knots.

ONBOARD LOCATION COUNTS

In general, the most comfortable location on any boat is about half to two-thirds of the way aft, near the location of the longitudinal center of gravity (LCG) and the longitudinal center of buoyancy (LCB). That is where the pitching motion is least and the roll motion is smaller. In an ideal world, the owner's stateroom, the galley, and the bridge would all be located there, but that, of course, is impossible: the bridge must be farther forward for better visibility, and the owner's stateroom is often placed farther aft or forward for privacy. (Did you know that the term *stateroom* comes from the early days of Mississippi River steamers, when their great cabins were named after various states, with the largest room being the Texas?)

Because the LCB in slower vessels is just aft of amidships, the heaviest weights—namely the engines—are usually located there, with the saloon above them. In heavy weather, the saloon experiences minimal motion in this location, and remains comfortable when the ends of the boat are not. In general, faster boats have their engines farther aft, with very high-speed deep-V boats having them just forward of the transom. Notice that on ultra-high-speed boats the helm position is almost directly over the center of buoyancy, giving the person at the helm and the crew the best location for a soft ride.

STABILIZERS

To make the ride even easier in a larger, slower boat, stabilizers can be fitted, but only on displacement hull shapes. Stabilizers can be active or passive. Active stabilizers look like small stubby wings sticking out of the lower part of the hull, just below the waterline. Passive stabilizers can be bilge keels, a centerline keel, or flume tanks on either side of the boat.

PASSIVE STABILIZERS

Passive stabilizers soften the rolling from side to side. The centerline keel was discussed at length in chapter 2. Bilge or twin keels also help slow the roll period of the hull and make the motion on deck and in the cabins more comfortable.

A flume tank or antiroll tank is another long-known method of slowing the roll of a boat, but it takes some time and experimentation to set up properly. Basically, antiroll tanks are located on either side of the hull. A pipe connects the tanks, and as the boat heels to one side, water surges through the pipe to the "downhill" tank. The pipe should be just small enough to delay that flow, with the length of the delay equaling the roll period of the hull. Thus, water fills the lower tank as it is rolling back up, damping the roll.

ACTIVE STABILIZERS

For a vessel to use active stabilizers, it must be underway. Water passes over the stabilizer wings and generates lift, just as an airplane wing does. As the boat rolls to port, for example, the port side of the hull goes down and forward. At the same time, a gyro senses the heel angle and automatically adjusts the stabilizer to counteract the rolling motion. The lift generated by the stabilizer acts against the roll and returns the boat to a level condition. In general, the faster a boat is moving, the easier it is for active stabilizers to counter the roll, but they only work on nonplaning hulls.

Active stabilizers can be used on slow to moderate-speed hulls, both round-bottomed and chined, but they are most often seen on larger round-bottomed yachts because round hulls tend to roll slightly more than chine hulls and because space is

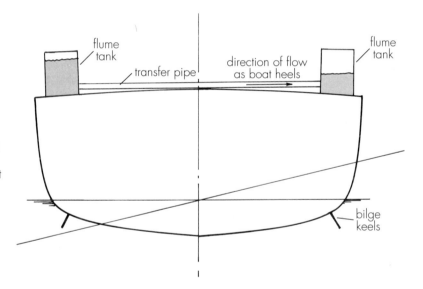

Flume tanks reduce roll by allowing water to flow from one side of the boat to the other. The transfer pipe must be correctly sized so that water flows at the right speed to dampen the roll. On the latest boats, flume tank flow is controlled by a computer. Note that this boat also has bilge keels.

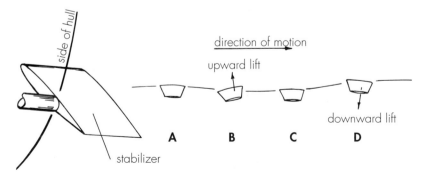

A stabilizer is like a mini-wing protruding through the side of the hull. As the vessel rolls, the stabilizer works to oppose and dampen the rolling motion.

available to fit the gyros and motors required to drive active stabilizers.

On fishing boats and some passagemaking yachts you might see flopper stoppers. These towed lifting devices, often triangular in shape, are suspended from either side of the vessel on wires at the ends of long booms. The flopper stopper seeks to maintain a constant depth and attitude to the sea's surface, and is said to "sail." Its resistance to upward movement counterbalances the roll of the hull. Flopper stoppers are only seen—and rarely so—on long-distance passagemaking yachts because they add drag, though they are common on deep-sea commercial fishing vessels.

PARAVANES

Underway, steel paravanes can enhance stability and slow heavy rolling. When trailed in the water, hydrodynamic lifting forces keep them deeply submerged. This lift force (acting downward) helps to slow the boat's roll and enhance stability. Like flopper stoppers, the vanes are suspended from the ends of booms to get them outboard far enough. Their efficiency depends on being well outboard of the boat and deep enough in the water so that they cannot be pulled to the surface. Shaped something like a torpedo with wings, paravanes are more popular than flopper stoppers, but they do tend to slow the boat down and have been known to snag floating objects and unexpectedly heel the boat over.

DYNAMIC STABILIZATION

Planing hulls use dynamic stabilization to remain upright in a seaway. In other words, dynamic lift tends to be balanced across the entire hull and keeps the boat level until high seas upset the equilibrium. It is this phenomenon that makes deep-V hulls stable at speed, whereas they often exhibit a pronounced roll when drifting or moving at displacement speeds. Dynamic stabilization, however, is difficult to quantify at the design stage, although computer programs are beginning to address the problem. Dynamic stabilization assumes that the hull is fully and evenly supported across its surface. This is true enough in calm water, but when the waves get up, care needs to be taken to ensure that the boat stays on course when it slams down on a wave crest and uneven lift develops.

COMFORT ON DECK

Being comfortable on deck is not just about lying on a sun pad and enjoying a cool beverage, although that is an enjoyable pastime. On a comfortable deck you can go forward safely, climb to the flybridge easily and safely, and move around the cockpit without feeling as if you might fall over the side. You are at ease driving the boat, and your passengers are comfortable sitting in the cockpit or on the bridge.

EASY AND SAFE TO GO FORWARD

I once went forward from the cockpit to the foredeck on a 50-foot (15 m) boat while it was making 30 knots into a moderate sea. The foredeck was huge and flat, but apart from the bow rail there were no handholds. Walking to the anchor windlass and anchor was hazardous, though the clean foredeck made the boat look sleek and extremely modern. Too often, marketing departments drive yacht design, and their considerations often do not include basic safety features. Frankly, I would have preferred a safer and less sleek boat with handholds and perhaps some structures to brace against.

If you anchor off or need to go forward regularly—you might fish off the bow, or need to tend docklines—your foredeck should have handholds. A good handhold on a small boat can take the form of a single rail about 6 inches (15 cm) off the deck running from the cabin side to the bow. On a larger boat it could be a single middeck rail, but the cabinhouse must have enough handrails on it to allow you to reach the middeck rail while you are still holding on somewhere else. On still larger boats the bow rails are usually a minimum of 24 inches (61 cm) high, but this catches most people right behind the knees. Much safer are 28- to 30-inch rails (71–76 cm). The old saying, "One hand for yourself, one for the boat," means that no matter where you are on the boat, there should be something secure to grab for support.

Back in the cockpit, there should be handholds in furniture and around any discontinuities in the cabin sole—that is, near a step or ladder. Handholds should continue throughout the entire boat. Boats, whether they are slow or fast, get tossed around by waves, and strong handholds are your best insurance against injury.

Easy-to-Climb Ladders and Stairwells

Ladders cause more problems in boats than almost any other feature. In my opinion, ladders to the flybridge need to have side rails to hold onto. People unused to going up a ladder hold onto the rungs as they climb; but rungs should be wide enough for large feet and therefore should be too wide for gripping. Also, if you hold onto rungs instead of side rails, the person descending the ladder immediately after you might step on your fingers.

The most important part of the ladder is the hatch at the top. The best ladder rails run up past floor level so you can step off the ladder onto the bridge sole. If the ladder ends at sole level, you will need handholds to pull yourself upright. The best designs incorporate a rail around the

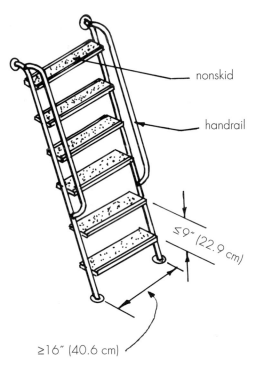

nonskid

handrail

≤9" (22.9 cm)

≥16" (40.6 cm)

A properly sized ladder is safer to climb or descend. Rungs should not be spaced more than 9 inches (23 cm) apart and the ladder should not be less than 16 inches (41 cm) wide. Good handrails and nonskid on the treads help make this ladder even safer.

hatch to prevent someone from walking down the wrong side of the hatch. (Going down the wrong side will make your eyes water!)

Stairwells also need handholds and properly spaced stairs. Often stairs are spaced too closely together or steps are too short to safely walk up and down.

Easy to Work in the Cockpit or to Enjoy the Fantail

The first requirement for enjoying the deck aft is that the boat not pitch too much. Severe pitching makes the ends of the boat uncomfortable. Pitching is a function of sea state and hull characteristics. In general, a boat with fine ends and plenty of beam amidships will tend to pitch more than a boat with a fat transom stern and a moderately fine bow.

The second requirement is that the layout be suitable. All too often seats are not properly shaped before they are molded. Current standards suggest that widths be about 20 inches (51 cm). Note how the seat back in the accompanying illustration slopes backward at the ideal slope of 8 to 1.

Fewer Steps between Deck Levels

One of the easiest ways to fall overboard is to trip over a small step. Steps at least 8 inches (20 cm) high rarely cause problems, but steps that rise less than 3 inches (7.5 cm) are easily missed in the dark, resulting in tripping or falling. When inspecting a boat, make sure that there are no short steps. Often a slight ramp clues you in that the sole is uneven rather than a low step.

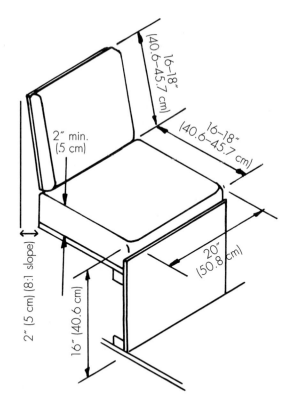

Seats should be sized to suit human dimensions. This seat will be quite comfortable if it adheres to the dimensions shown.

LIGHTING FOR COMFORT

You sit in a comfortable chair, ready to relax after a day's cruise. Someone comes into the saloon and switches on the lights. One overhead light illuminates your seat, and its glare is annoying. You try to ignore it, but no matter how you twist in your seat, you can't avoid the glare. You try to adjust the light, but it's fixed in place, so you turn it off. Now you sit in semidarkness. One irritating light means that you can no longer enjoy your favorite chair.

Lights should be unobtrusive—that is, they should not attract your eye or shine directly at you. Reading lights should be located behind and slightly to one side of you so they illuminate the page without shining into your face. Overhead lights are best if they are dimmable and recessed or very low profile. Nothing is quite so annoying as having to duck around a light fixture every time you walk through a cabin. Ideally, light fixtures should be placed clear of walkways. This usually puts them above furniture or on vertical walls. Switches should be to hand, but not in areas where you are likely to brush against them or accidentally turn them on.

I also like to see a few red lights for nighttime use (especially near doorways leading to the deck) and under-furniture microlights or rope lights to illuminate walkways. The bridge definitely should have red overhead lights to enable the person at the helm to retain night vision so he or she can see where the boat is headed. All bridge instruments should have red or green lights with dimmer switches.

DECK LIGHTING

On deck the lighting needs to be bright enough to illuminate the immediate area. Walkways, steps, and stairs should be brightly lit with red lights or dimmers for nighttime use. Frankly, at sea I prefer to have red lights rather than bright overhead lights illuminating steps. For pleasant evenings at anchor or in port you should have white overhead lights.

Areas on deck where regular activity will take place should be well lit. For example, the cockpit of a sportfisherman should be brightly illuminated when needed to allow anglers to see their lines

and gear. The area around the anchor and windlass also should be brightly lit when needed to ensure that the anchor operator can see what is happening with the anchor, rode, any markers set, orientation of the boat, etc.

Some areas of the boat require dual-purpose lighting. For example, a cruising boat might have a dining table on the afterdeck, requiring a fairly bright light for setting up and a lower lighting level for dining. In this case, a dimmer or lower-intensity lighting circuit may be fitted.

You can set the mood for a pleasant evening with adjustable lighting circuits. Lights that cause glare or eyestrain can ruin a good evening. The right lighting improves the atmosphere aboard your boat and increases your comfort level without being expensive or even noticeable.

LIGHTING IN THE ENGINE ROOM

Good engine room lighting is essential. On many boats the engine compartment is deep within the hull and without hatches or windows to let in daylight. Consequently, bright fluorescent lighting is required to allow the engineer (who might be you) to see all around the engine room and engines. You might want one or two cable lights for awkward spots.

Fluorescent lights give good strong white light without generating much heat. If you have to work in close proximity to a light for any length of time, don't use an incandescent or high-intensity light because of the high temperatures they produce. A fluorescent light on a cable allows you to position the light exactly where you need it. Have a second work light available in case you drop the first.

INTERIOR COMFORT

For the yacht designer and interior designer, selecting the right furniture dimensions to suit the owners and crew is not an easy task. For example, let's say the boat is intended to seat three or four people at the dining table. A normal person fills about 18 to 20 inches (46–51 cm) of width on a seat, so the seat could be 80 inches (2 m) wide to suit four people. Anyone who has had to sit in the middle of three airline seats knows that sitting between two people for any length of time is not very enjoyable. Consequently, we should probably reduce the number of people to three

and make the seat about 74 inches (1.88 m) long to give each person some elbow room. A typical bunk is 74 to 76 inches (188–193 cm) long, so the seat also could be used for sleeping. But if the seat is to be used as a bunk, as it often is in the forepeak of a smaller boat, we have a width problem. The minimum width of a bunk should be 30 to 36 inches (76–91 cm), and a seat should only be 18 inches (46 cm) deep. What to do? The seat can be made to fit into 36 inches (91 cm) by building a removable seatback with a 6-inch (15 cm) deep cushion. This leaves a 10-inch (25 cm) space for a locker in which to stow bedding and pillows.

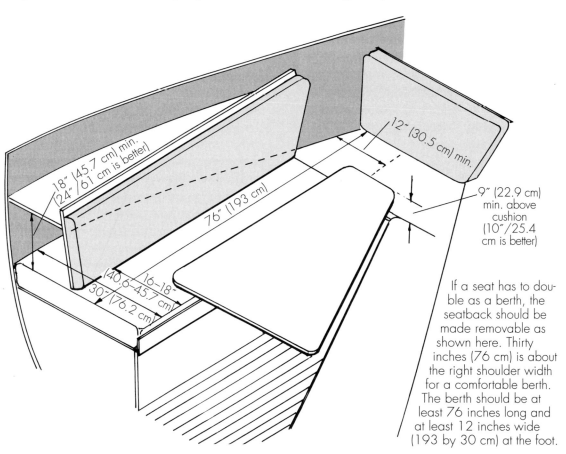

18" (45.7 cm) min. (24"/61 cm is better)

76" (193 cm)

12" (30.5 cm) min.

9" (22.9 cm) min. above cushion (10"/25.4 cm is better)

16–18" (40.6–45.7 cm)

30" (76.2 cm)

If a seat has to double as a berth, the seatback should be made removable as shown here. Thirty inches (76 cm) is about the right shoulder width for a comfortable berth. The berth should be at least 76 inches long and at least 12 inches wide (193 by 30 cm) at the foot.

Most people don't sit erect, however, preferring to slouch or lounge. When people slouch they take up less height, but they spread out more. Seats made to suit body contours will be uncomfortable when the occupant slouches or lounges. Thick cushions allow a user to adopt any posture without becoming uncomfortable. Cushions should be a minimum of 2 inches (50 mm) thick, but 3- or even 4-inch (75–100 mm) cushions are more comfortable.

When designing seats, more than the actual sitting area needs to be considered. Foot space needs to be addressed, especially at the helm station. Ideally, a foot space of 12 to 16 inches (30–40 cm) is required. If the seat is placed lower, more foot space will be needed because people will stretch out a little more.

Height also is critical. A comfortable seat is about 17 inches (43 cm) above floor level, and the seatback should be 18 inches (46 cm) high or higher. A seated person is about 36 inches (91 cm) tall.

Just getting standing headroom is often difficult on smaller boats. For example, if a cuddy cabin with full headroom is required, the designer may have to resort to tricks with the sheerline and the cabintop to achieve that goal. The accompanying drawing shows a possible solution. Achieving the required cabin height, however, is not the end of the problem. The person at the helm needs to see over the cabintop when seated, which often means that the helm must be raised. The end result may be an unwieldy design that needs a longer hull to get the right proportions.

A lesser problem aboard boats is often the location of a TV or video screen. Ideally, such a screen should be directly in front of the user, with the user's eye level at about one third down from the top of the screen. Aboard many boats, TV sets are placed on high shelves, forcing a watcher to lean back and slouch even more than normal.

A computer screen should be lower still; the user's eye height should be near the

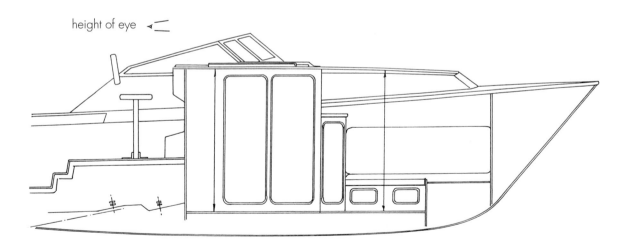

In designing the bridge or cabin, the height of the helmsman's eye is important. In this partial view of one of the author's designs, the helm seat is raised to allow a clear line of sight forward over the cabintop.

top of the viewable area, and the screen should be 20 inches (51 cm) or more from the user.

DOORS, PASSAGEWAYS, AND WALKWAYS

What is the narrowest door you can walk through without turning sideways? For most people the minimum is 20 inches (51 cm). Unfortunately, some boats have 18-inch-wide (46 cm) doorway widths, and on one boat I measured a door just 16 inches (41 cm) wide! Even slender people will find it difficult to move through doors this narrow.

The ideal minimum width for doors and passageways should be about 24 inches (61 cm), with 36 inches (91 cm) being the widest. If a passageway is much wider than 36 inches, a person could be bounced off the walls when the boat hits a wave. On wider passageways, handrails should be provided at wrist or belt height.

BRIDGE LAYOUT

Laying out a bridge is one of the most difficult jobs a designer faces, primarily because of its location in the boat. Ideally, the bridge should be near the front of the engine room so that controls can be routed to the engine with minimum difficulty. By making the control systems simple to maintain, a designer or builder is better assured that maintenance will in fact occur. Unfortunately, the bridge is usually some distance ahead of the engine compartment and controls have to be fitted in a trunk leading to the ER.

The helm station must have visibility down both sides of the boat. It also needs to be located with instruments easily visible and controls at hand. The person at the helm must be able to sit or stand in comfort.

A few basic parameters start the layout process. If the wheel is on centerline, visibility is reasonable on both sides of the boat (a foot recess should be built in to allow a person to stand close to the wheel). On larger yachts, a remote helm station or auxiliary autopilot is often located on the bridge wings to give the person at the helm better visibility during docking maneuvers.

The helm seat can be mounted 17 inches (43 cm) behind the wheel, which is just enough space to let the person at the helm stand or sit. With a sliding seat, he or she gains more room. If the wheel and seat are raised a foot or so (provided there is adequate headroom), visibility is improved. Placing the compass, radar, video screens, dials and other instruments immediately in front of the person at the helm makes them easy to read. They should be distributed above and below the windshield so as not to obstruct the view from the helm, and organized by use, with those used most frequently placed most conveniently. Throttles and gearshifts need to be within reach of the helm at all times, but they can be mounted to one side of the dials. Switches can be placed around the edges of the center console.

The navigation table should be placed near the helm station. Despite the growing popularity of electronic chart displays, the U.S. Coast Guard still recommends that boats have paper charts onboard. Paper charts require a chart table large enough to hold them, even if the boat has a chart plotter or computer-based charting system.

Remember, too, that the boat will go astern. Consequently, on boats with enclosed bridges there should be windows in the aft side; if not, the person at the helm should be able to walk out onto the bridge wing to see aft. Some sportfishermen have a remote helm aft for use when fighting a fish.

SLEEPING QUARTERS

Choosing a place to sleep is simple: take the nearest empty bunk . . . or should you? Ideally, the best bunks are nearest the middle of the boat, where motion is least. Bunks forward tend to get bouncy as the boat slams into waves. Bunks aft tend to be noisy because they are over the props. Engine and exhaust noise also can make aft bunks hard to sleep in, although motion is gentler aft than forward, especially in a transom-stern vessel.

Bunks should be oriented with the occupant's head toward the bow, because a boat trims up by the bow, and you don't want to sleep head down. I am not a fan of athwartship bunks, which are best when used in harbor, but at sea the bunk tilts sideways as the bow trims up, and if the boat makes a turn, centrifugal force shoves the occupant to one end.

Bunks on an angle offer the worst of all worlds. If you try to sleep head-up in a narrow forward berth, you end up rolling out unless the bunk is fitted with lee cloths. If the boat heels in a turn, you roll out. If the boat accelerates, you slide downward and out. If the boat slows or stops, you are squished into the head end of the bunk.

BUNK DIMENSIONS

What is the ideal width of a bunk? Frankly, I like to be reasonably snug so I won't roll around as the boat banks into a turn or flies off a wave. A snug bunk is 28 to 30 inches (71–76 cm) wide at the shoulder, 18 to 20 inches (46–51 cm) at the foot. It is at least 6 feet, 4 inches (193 cm) long and has a 3- to 4-inch (76–102 mm) cushion or mattress of reasonably hard foam. If the foam is too thin, your hip will "bottom out" on the bunk bottom, which could keep you awake all night. Wider bunks are more comfortable but allow you to roll around too much when the boat is underway. Double bunks are too wide for sleeping unless the boat is in harbor and there is relatively little motion.

BATHROOMS AND TOILETS

Small compartments such as the shower and the head need careful design. At a minimum, a person showering will need a space at least 28 inches (711 mm) square. If the shower is combined with a toilet or water closet, the space must be increased to about 42 by 30 inches (106 by 76 cm). As boat size increases, more space can be allocated to the head and shower unit, even to the point of including a bath or whirlpool.

On a slightly larger boat, additional features such as towel racks, grab rails, a hamper, a washbasin, lockers, and even a vanity might be included in the head. On smaller boats it often takes an ingenious designer to fit many of these features. On open boats, of course, these features are just a wish and a dream. But center-console boats increasingly have a WC in the center console.

DESIGNING FOR GOOD MAINTENANCE

Although maintenance is not an obvious comfort factor, it does give you peace of mind to know that a boat's systems are properly cared for. In order to maintain the boat as it was intended, you need access to the parts that need changing, upgrading, or checking.

In a twin-engine installation, both engines should have hatches or other means of access to all sides of the engine. If that is not possible, there at least should be access to the engine filters and dipsticks for the engine and transmission. When looking over the engine for maintenance, make sure all belts and hoses can be easily inspected. That way you will be sure to notice when one is about to break.

The shaft logs must be accessible, too, in case they begin to leak or need tightening. Quite often shaft logs are located under or very close to the back of the engine. If this is the case, it is often worth looking at other types of shaft logs that reduce maintenance.

Batteries should be mounted in bolted-down, acid-proof boxes (with lids to prevent metal objects from accidentally bridging the terminals), and isolated with a switch when they are not in use. They must be accessible for checking electrolyte levels.

Remember to wire the electric bilge pump directly to the battery terminals rather than wiring it on the other side of the isolation switch (i.e., the battery 1-2-both-off switch). If you wire the bilge pump on the far side of the isolation switch, you turn off the bilge pump when the switch is turned off, which means that the bilge pump is turned off when you leave the boat. Rather, you want to leave a bilge pump (as well as the float switch that turns on the pump when water levels reach a certain height) operational in case a leak occurs or heavy rain finds its way aboard after you've left the boat.

Pumps and compressors should be located where they can be visually inspected on a regular basis. All too often a pump or compressor is jammed into any available corner, where it may be forgotten until it breaks down or the belt snaps. Pumps need regular lubrication and belt tensioning.

As with just about everything else that moves on a boat, the steering gear should be checked fairly often. I have been aboard relatively new boats where parts of the steering gear were rusted, simply because the gear was not visible when the lazarette hatch was opened and so was not inspected. If the gear can be easily seen, the hydraulic rams can be lubricated periodically, the hoses and hose connections inspected for corrosion, the reservoir topped up, and the rudderstock bearings checked. The same applies to other types of steering—cable, rack-and-pinion, etc. (see chapter 11). Accessible gear encourages preventive maintenance that will prevent sudden catastrophic failures.

Bilge pumps, too, should be accessible through a convenient hatch in the cabin sole. If the pump is located under a screwed-down cabin sole and clogs, you may not be able to pump the bilge. That's a dumb way to lose a boat. I prefer at least two bilge pumps onboard: an engine-driven pump and an electric pump in the bilge. A backup hand-operated third pump with a long length of hose attached to the intake allows you to pump out inaccessible areas that might not drain into the main sump.

STORAGE

If you power off a wave and your VHF comes crashing down from its shelf or slides off a bunk because there was no place to stow it, you are going to be pretty mad at yourself for losing expensive electronics. Having enough storage space allows gear to be properly stowed.

Good storage includes hanging lockers for outerwear, a lockable cabinet for electronic gear, bins for clothes, galley lockers for food, cutlery, and crockery, and underbunk stowage for larger pieces of gear. On a sportfisherman it might include live baitwells and ice chests. On a trawler-style yacht it might include engine room storage for tools and engine spares. It might also include fixed storage for the anchor and rode.

ELECTRONICS STORAGE

Generally, electronic equipment is located on the bridge, although stereo and TV systems may be in the saloon. The major criterion when fitting electronic gear is to locate it where it will not get overheated, wet, or bounced around. This means that electronics should not be located in the engine compartment and probably not in the galley. Also locate them away from windows that open.

In general, the accelerations that most boats experience are not high enough to affect marine electronics as long as all terminals and plugs are screwed in properly.

GALLEY STORAGE

There never seems to be enough storage space in the galley, especially on long cruises. Most storage space in the galley is used for utensils, dishware, pots and pans, and food. Allocate dedicated storage areas for each item. Storage for dishware should keep pots and pans from moving around and breaking. Storage for food must restrain packages. Cramming a lot of items into one space prevents "soft" foods such as rice, flour, and grains, from shifting.

For loose items I prefer to use clear plastic containers, which won't break, causing a mess or a glass hazard, and which allow you to see what is inside without opening the lid. The best types go directly from freezer to microwave without having to remove the contents. Maximize galley space by building racks to store plastic containers.

LOCKERS

Decide what equipment will go in each locker (you may want to label lockers). Rather than hang cups on racks, put them in a locker. Make sure that knives are stowed in a drawer or fastened down in a knife rack and that the rack keeps them secure.

Lockers for clothes need to be wide enough to hold folded clothes, which usually means they should be at least 16 inches (41 cm) across. Hanging lockers need to hold a coat hanger, which requires about 18 inches (46 cm) of width.

REFRIGERATOR

Refrigerate food as you would at home. With a small refrigerator, however, you may have to be more selective. You might keep soft drinks in a portable cooler in the cockpit rather than in the refrigerator.

Under the Cabin Sole

Canned goods can be stowed in the bilge, provided it's not running with old oil. Adding weight here lowers the center of gravity and opens extra space in the galley. A friend who spends considerable time fishing offshore always keeps a few cans of stew in the bilge, just in case he runs out of real food.

Overhead Storage

Just as you would on an airplane, save overhead storage for lighter gear. If storage is at a premium, use undercabinet nets to hold items such as daily newspapers (some get ink over everything) and magazines. Nets hung above the galley are great for storing lengths of sausage, salami, cheeses, fruit, and other goodies.

Engine Room Storage

In the engine compartment on small boats, stowage often is limited, but on boats with a little more space, engine spares, lubricating oil, and transmission oil can be stored in the engine compartment. If you cannot stow gear in the engine compartment—even though it is large enough—use noncombustible materials to construct a storage box, but make sure it is at least 10 inches (25 cm) from the hot exhaust and from moving parts. Also make sure it cannot come loose and fall into the engine, where it may do damage. Never store extra fuel in the engine compartment.

Anchor Storage

I was once powering into a strong head sea when the anchor on the bow roller came loose. A sharp edge on the anchor roller had cut through the cord we had used to lash down the anchor. The anchor flew upward with such a force that it bent the underside of the bow rail and put a hole in the deck where it landed. The lesson learned was that no matter how well you think you have lashed an anchor, it can come adrift and do serious damage.

Anchors should be stored where they cannot come adrift—either in an anchor locker, lashed down to pads belowdecks, or secured to the bow roller.

Anchor lockers are purpose-built for the job, but the anchor, once inside the locker, should be securely tied down. Unsecured anchors have flown out of the locker and disappeared over the side, along with the anchor locker lid.

Anchors stowed belowdecks also need to be tied down. The best method uses wooden chocks or pads in combination with eyebolts fiberglassed to the hull. Set the anchor on the pads, lash it, and it will stay secure. Don't let an anchor simply lie in a locker. As soon as you head out to sea, it can and usually will attack the nearest piece of furniture. I know an owner who left an anchor on the cabin sole when his boat was being delivered overland by truck. When the truck went around corners, the anchor slammed against furniture on either side of the hull. When the truck braked, the anchor slid forward and smashed against a bulkhead. The repair job took the boat out of commission for several weeks and cost the owner a lot of money.

The bow roller should have a hole through which an anchor can be pinned. If it doesn't, lash the anchor. Before you head to sea, though, make sure the bow roller has no sharp edges that might cut through any lashings.

There are many ways to increase storage space on a boat: you just have to use your imagination and remember where you stowed the stuff. Conscientious owners record the location of all stowed items in the ship's logbooks.

Comfort, as we have seen, can mean many things. Some, such as cushions and seat shapes, are straightforward. Others, such as anchor and chain stowage, are not so obvious, but without them your journey becomes harder and could end up damaging the boat.

POWERING YOUR BOAT

WHAT'S THE BEST type of engine to power a boat? Inboard or outboard, gas or diesel? Conventional propeller shaft, sterndrive, or jet drive? It depends a great deal on the boat; generally, the designer specs the type and size of engines at the same time he or she is drawing the boat.

There are, however, choices for owners to make. If it's to be an outboard, should you have a conventional two-stroke, a four-stroke, or one of the newer, high-tech units with names like Bombardier's Evinrude Ficht fuel injection, Mercury's Optimax, or Yamaha's HPDI?

What are the pros and cons of sterndrives and inboards in terms of maintenance performance and cost? Certainly there are many terms to understand.

Engines have come a long way in the last hundred years—even the last twenty —and now manufacturers are concerned about the year 2006 federal emissions regulations to which all engines will have to conform. These approaching regulations and the new technologies to meet them have ushered in many changes and will continue to do so.

EARLY ENGINES

The earliest boat engines were steam powered, but for the boats we're interested in, gasoline or diesel engines are now the practical choices. (Steam engines have been relegated to large ships, and even there are losing ground to modern diesels.) Modern engines are almost universally *internal combustion*, meaning that the fuel is burned inside the power-developing cylinder as opposed to creating steam in a boiler with an external flame.

Lenoire built the first production internal combustion engine in Paris in 1860. (Its predecessors included a number of experimental internal-combustion engines going back as far as Christian Huygens's gunpowder-fueled engine of 1680, but Lenoire produced the first commercial engine.) This engine had a single horizontal cylinder with combustion on either side of the piston, and it could generate a few horsepower.

The next big step along the road of progress was an analysis of the combustion cycle by Otto in Germany in 1876. Otto determined that an engine cycle should have four distinct phases or piston strokes: induction, compression, expansion, and exhaust. Later that year the N. A. Otto Company built the first four-stroke engine. More efficient and quieter than earlier engines, it established the norm for four-stroke engines. The following year, Dugald Clerk of Scotland obtained a patent for a two-stroke engine. Clerk's engine was fueled by coal gas injected into the crankcase and valved into the cylinder.

Like Clerk's engine, Lenoire's engine and early Otto engines burned gaseous fuel such as illuminating gas. This discouraged mobile use. In 1883 Karl Benz made an engine with a carburetor that could burn a mobile, easily handled liquid petroleum fuel, and the world hasn't been the same since.

In Germany in 1889, Dr. Rudolph Diesel received a patent for his engine idea. It took five more years for him to sell the idea to Krupp and Sulzer and develop an engine. This engine was a single upright cylinder with a bore of 150 mm (5.9 in.) and a stroke of 400 mm (15.75 in.). The cylinder shell was made of cast steel with cast-iron walls. The piston had bronze rings, but as it heated the rings expanded at a rate different from steel's expansion rate and so were eventually replaced with steel rings. The engine flywheel was 1.2 meters (about 4 ft.) in diameter. The first injector (known as an *atomizer*) was at the top of the cylinder, along with a dual-intake valve, an air starting and charging valve, and an adjustable safety valve. Numerous teething problems were gradually eliminated. For example, the cylinder was cast about 60 percent larger than Diesel calculated and only yielded a pressure of 310 psi. A new cylinder allowed the pressure to rise to 1,160 psi and blew the top off the engine, the pieces narrowly missing Diesel and his helpers. From the prototype to production took two more years, and it wasn't until 1895 that the Rational Heat Engine with Fuel Pump Attached, as Diesel called it, was put into production. It was an instant success, though too large and heavy at first for vehicles, and it made Rudolph Diesel a rich man. Unfortunately, he made bad investments, lost most of his money, and died virtually broke in 1913.

BASIC ENGINE TYPES

TWO-STROKE CYCLE OR "TWO-CYCLE" ENGINES (GASOLINE)

The two-stroke cycle used today is similar to that developed by Clerk more than a hundred years ago. The charge of fuel-air mixture is inducted into the crankcase as the piston rises. As the piston descends on its power stroke, a valve closes off the crankcase inlet and the charge is compressed in the crankcase. As the piston nears the bottom of its stroke, it uncovers an inlet port in the cylinder wall, allowing the charge to flow into the cylinder. The rising piston then closes off the inlet port and the somewhat higher exhaust port, compressing the fuel-air mixture. A fraction of a second before the piston reaches top dead center (TDC), the fuel is ignited by the spark from the spark plug and burns extremely rapidly. This rapid burn—call it an explosion—forces the piston downward again. As the piston descends the exhaust port uncovers, allowing the burned gases to escape. The piston continues to descend, uncovering

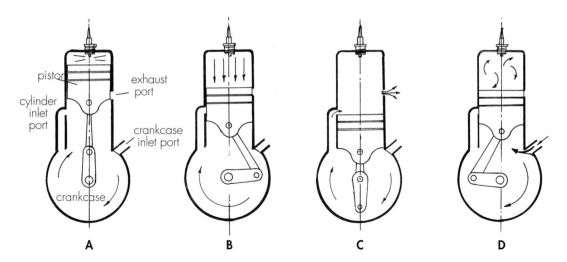

The two-stroke cycle in a gasoline engine. **A** shows the piston at top dead center (TDC) as the fuel is ignited. The exploding gases force the piston downward until the exhaust port is opened. It also compresses the new charge of fuel in the crankcase. When the exhaust port opens (**B**), the burned gases are vented out. As the piston descends even lower to **C**, a new fuel charge is allowed to enter by exposing the cylinder inlet port. The new fuel charge is compressed as the piston rises again (**D**) and then it is ignited as in **A**.

the inlet port, it allows another charge of fuel and air to flow into the cylinder, and the cycle repeats. In the two-stroke cycle, the engine fires every time the piston reaches TDC; in other words, there is one revolution of the crankshaft per combustion cycle.

The greatest advantage of the two-stroke is its simplicity. It requires none of the complex valve-operating hardware of the four-stroke, and two-stroke engines are generally smaller, lighter, and less expensive than comparable four-strokes. This has made them the traditional choice for outboard engines. A two-stroke engine also develops more torque than a four-stroke of equal horsepower, because work is done on every stroke.

The problems with two-strokes have been that they pollute more than similarly sized four-strokes, they burn more fuel,

and they make more noise. The pollution concern arises from the fact that the engine's lubricating oil is mixed with the gas for delivery to the cylinder, where it undergoes incomplete combustion and is thereafter exhausted to the environment. This problem has been greatly reduced by current oils, which can be added to the fuel in a volume ratio as small as 2 percent (for a 50:1 fuel-oil mixture) or less, and by automatic oil metering systems. A continuing problem, causing both pollution and higher fuel consumption, is that as the fresh fuel-air mixture is drawn into the combustion cylinder, some of it spills out the exhaust port under pressure. This results in hydrocarbon emissions and a loss of efficiency. But new two-stroke engines offer some innovative solutions to this problem.

Four-Stroke Cycle or "Four-Cycle" Engines (Gasoline)

Four-stroke engines still work on the Otto cycle. In the induction stroke, the downward-moving piston pulls a charge of fuel and air into the cylinder through the open intake valve. On the compression stroke, the intake and exhaust valves close and the piston starts on its upward journey, compressing the charge. As the piston reaches TDC, the spark plug fires and the expanding gases push the piston down the cylinder. This is the expansion or working stroke. At the end of the expansion stroke the exhaust valve opens and the exhaust gases vent from the cylinder. The piston then travels back up the cylinder while the exhaust valve stays open. This exhaust stroke has the effect of blowing the exhaust gases out of the cylinder. Then the cycle repeats as the piston descends, the exhaust valve closes, the intake opens, and a new charge of fuel-air mixture is inducted. The cycle is thus completed every two revolutions of the crankshaft.

The advantages of a four-stroke engine are that the mechanically controlled valves, the separation of the intake from exhaust strokes, and the separation of lubricating oil from the fuel give better control of the fuel charge, resulting in less pollution, higher efficiency, and less noise.

The disadvantage is that these valves require complex operating systems, with a camshaft driven off the crankshaft to synchronize the valve openings with the engine's rotation at all speeds. Four-stroke engines are therefore generally bigger, heavier, and more expensive than two-stroke engines. Most inboard gasoline engines are four-stroke, and a growing number of outboards are, as well.

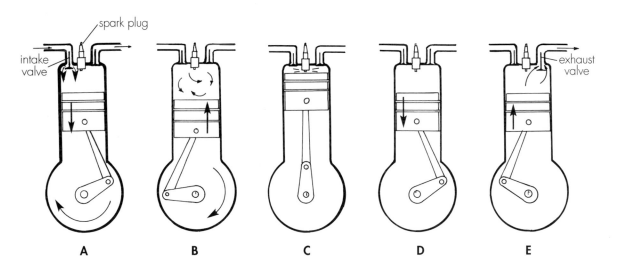

The four-stroke gasoline-engine cycle. Fuel enters the combustion chamber through the intake valve (**A**). The piston then rises, compressing the fuel charge (**B**). The fuel charge is ignited at **C** and the piston is forced downward (**D**). On the return stroke the burned fuel is expelled through the exhaust valve (**E**). The piston then descends to bottom dead center and a new fuel charge is allowed in.

DIESEL ENGINES (INBOARDS)

New marine diesels in the size range used by most recreational boats are now all four-stroke engines. The venerable Detroit 6-71 and its cousins were two-strokes, but all Detroits are now four-strokes, like the rest. Two-stroke diesels are used on ships, but they are as big as a house—sometimes a very large house!

Diesels operate on the same four-stroke cycle as gasoline engines, with several critical differences: on the intake stroke, only fresh air is ingested. The air charge is compressed to a much higher pressure than in the gasoline engine, which heats the air to a very high temperature. As the piston reaches the top, the fuel injector sprays a precisely metered mist of fuel directly into the superheated cylinder. These tiny droplets start to burn immediately, starting the expansion or working stroke. Diesels have no spark plugs; instead, they have fuel injectors.

The fuel injector is fed by a pump through which diesel fuel is constantly circulating. That is why on diesel engines there is a line taking fuel to the pump and a line returning fuel from the pump to the tank. It is critically important that air does not get into the fuel system, because if it does it can form an airlock that stops fuel getting to the engine. For this reason diesel engines are *bled*—that is, the fuel is allowed to run through the system until all air bubbles have been removed—before the fuel lines are bolted up tightly. So don't run them out of fuel.

Diesel engines have two main advantages: first, their high efficiency still exceeds that of gasoline engines. Second, diesel fuel is much less volatile than gasoline, and the risks of fire and explosion on board are therefore greatly reduced. The principal drawbacks of diesel engines are that their higher operating pressures require more robust construction, and the fuel injectors and pumps are expensive components that must be manufactured with extreme precision. Diesels are generally larger, heavier, and more expensive than gas engines, though recent advances reduce these disadvantages.

OUTBOARD ENGINES

An outboard engine, as its name implies, is outboard of the hull. It can be either a two- or four-stroke engine. Unlike an inboard engine, the cylinders in an outboard are horizontal and the engine crankshaft drives a vertical geared drive shaft that meshes with a horizontal geared shaft in the lower unit on which the prop is mounted. This configuration greatly simplifies the boat designer's job. With an outboard, the entire power train is simply bolted to the transom and the boat is ready to go. Outboards can be tipped up out of the water when the boat is not in use. Outboard-powered boats need no rudder aft of the prop, since the engine is turned to control the boat's direction. Consequently, with no through-hull steering gear, outboards tend to be easier to install.

A further advantage of outboards is that the engine can be trimmed to set the prop thrust parallel with the water's surface. This makes the thrust much more efficient and helps the boat run at a more level attitude.

Outboards are not without problems, however. One is that the length of the vertical drive shaft is limited by engineering considerations. In order to get the prop sufficiently low in the water, a transom cutout is often required. Transom cutouts lower a boat's freeboard at the stern and make it susceptible to swamping when the boat goes hard astern. An estimate by the insurance division of BoatU.S. states that in 13 of 15 boats surveyed to find out why they sank, a transom cutout was too low and caused the boat's sinking. If you have a boat with a transom cutout, make sure there is a secondary bulwark the same height as the top of the transom, inboard of the engine, as in the photo on page 40.

One way of preventing swamping is to mount the outboard on a bracket well aft of the transom (see for example, the photo on page 37). Not only does this eliminate a cutout, it helps to move engine thrust farther aft, which puts the propeller in cleaner water, making the prop more efficient.

RECENT OUTBOARD ENGINE DEVELOPMENTS

The U.S. Environmental Protection Agency (EPA) has mandated a reduction in engine emissions by the year 2006. Because of their traditional use of two-stroke engines, outboard manufacturers are much affected (manufacturers of two-stroke engines for snowmobiles, motorcycles, chain saws, lawn mowers, and weed cutters are also affected), and are responding with changes in technology. Because unburned fuel comprises much of the emissions from small two-stroke engines, designing the engines to burn fuel more efficiently not only makes them cleaner but also can increase their power and even make them run quieter. Outboard manufacturers have employed various technologies for cleaner-burning engines, but most use a combination of high-pressure fuel injection and computer-guided electronic systems and sensors.

Some companies, like Honda, have taken a different tack, forsaking two-strokes for the inherently cleaner-burning four-stroke, which are becoming available in an increasingly wider range of sizes.

Outboard engines have evolved far beyond anything Clerk or Otto could have imagined, and the evolution will continue. For example, Yamaha's HPDI (high-pressure direct injection) engine reduces emissions by nearly 75 percent compared with more conventional engines, yet still has the power and zip of a conventional two-stroke.

Modern outboards are increasingly complex. No longer are outboard owners concerned only with points, plugs, and a small fuel pump. Now engine salespeople talk of the high-pressure bus, tuned manifolds, and fuel atomization patterns. All these features are designed to reduce emissions and increase engine output.

All this means that outboard engine choices are increasingly exciting—and bewildering. Except for Honda engines, which are exclusively four-stroke, the major manufacturers offer both two- and four-stroke engines. All have new, low-emission, high-tech two-strokes that, along with their four-strokes, meet the 2006 regulations.

In this brave new world, the longtime boater has to discard old habits of mind. Take, for example, the carburetor. This is the traditional device for mixing fuel and air in gasoline engines. In the carburetor, the incoming air passes through a venturi where fuel is atomized into the air, forming

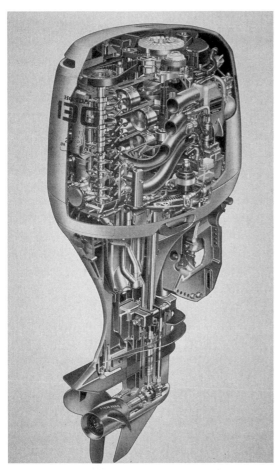

A cutaway view of Honda's 130 hp outboard shows how complex today's engines are. *(Honda Marine)*

into the cylinder. *Port injection* means that the nozzle is in the intake port, outside the cylinder proper. *Multiport injection* means that each cylinder of a multicylinder engine has a nozzle in its port. *EFI*, or electronic fuel injection, is a device that generally sprays fuel into the intake ports.

Direct fuel injection (DFI) means that the nozzle sprays fuel directly into the cylinder. *HPDI* (high-pressure direct injection) is promising new technology for gasoline engines. Direct injection allows two-strokes to inject fuel after the ports are closed, thus avoiding the loss of unburned fuel out the exhaust port, the traditional cause of pollution and high fuel consumption.

In all these injection schemes, the major gain is to bring the fuel distribution under electronic control. Various sensors monitor the engine's speed, load, temperature, and other parameters, and a microprocessor instantly adjusts the fuel delivery to suit. Not only are emissions reduced, but power, response, starting, and smoothness are improved.

(Diesel direct injection is a distinctly different system. The fuel is injected directly into the cylinder, as in HPDI, but the required pressures are higher—a few thousand pounds per square inch—to overcome the high compression pressures diesels generate. Also, the timing of the injection is critical, as it initiates the combustion. As in gas engines, many newer diesels are adopting computer controls for the injection.)

Yamaha's HPDI Two-Stroke Outboard Engine

On Yamaha's HPDI engines, sensors constantly monitor throttle position, ignition timing, rpm, water temperature, air temperature, atmospheric pressure, crank po-

a fuel-air mixture of the correct ratio. The carburetor also contains the throttle valve, which controls engine speed, and the choke, which enriches the mixture to aid cold starting. But on many larger engines, carburetors have been replaced by fuel injection. You can try looking for carburetors in the dealer's showroom, but you're not likely to find one on engines over 75 hp.

The term *fuel injection* applies to a number of devices that spray fuel under pressure sition, and the amount of O_2 (oxygen) in the exhaust gases. The microcomputer that reads the sensor output adjusts the ignition timing and fuel mixture to create the most efficient combustion. The O_2 sensor is unique to Yamaha; this patented device closes the loop from injecting the fuel to monitoring the exhaust gases for complete, efficient combustion.

The process starts when fuel is drawn through a filter pump and then pressurized to 700 psi. The pressurized fuel then goes through a vapor separator and into the fuel rail before it is injected into the cylinder in a finely atomized mist. According to Yamaha, this design increases efficiency over all rpm ranges, with the highest efficiency in the 2,500 to 5,000 rpm range. It features a new bottom piston ring designed to allow the proper amount of oil to lubricate the cylinder walls. According to Yamaha, in traditional direct-injection two-stroke engines the lubricating oil comes up from the bottom and the fuel enters at the top, a configuration that often starves the top piston rings of lubricant, leading to overheating and low life. In contrast, Yamaha's new piston ring design is supposed to allow the proper amount of oil past the ring for optimum lubrication. Formerly, the primary reason two-stroke engines polluted much more than four-strokes was that unburned fuel could slop out of the exhaust port. (Contrary to popular opinion, the burning of lubricating oil in 50:1 mixtures has been only a minor contributor to exhaust emissions in recent years.) The reason is that very little lubricating oil gets burned in the cylinder and what is burned is completely burned. Most pollution comes from the unburned hydrocarbons ejected after the two-stroke cycle, which leaves a telltale blue sheen on the water's surface.

Electronic Fuel Injection from Suzuki

Suzuki engines use sophisticated sensors mounted on the engine to feed information to an electronic control module (ECM). This information allows the ECM to inject precise amounts of fuel at high pressure into each cylinder. According to

Yamaha's new VZ150 hp high-pressure direct injected (HPDI) outboard—a 76 degree, 2.6 liter engine with superior fuel economy between 2,000 and 6,000 rpm—is representative of the latest breed of direct-injected two-stroke engines. *(Yamaha Motor Corp.)*

Suzuki's 25 hp four-stroke EFI outboard reliably powers this hunter's skiff on an early morning trip. *(Suzuki Motor Corp.)*

company literature, Suzuki was the first manufacturer to incorporate solid-state transistor ignition into an outboard engine. This ignition system increases spark strength and enables the spark to last longer for a cleaner burn. The four-stroke, three-cylinder, overhead cam, four-valve engines in the DF line (DF 25/30D, DF40/50, DF60/70, DF140) employ a large stroke and long bore to maximize power and torque at low speeds. These engines use an enclosed, oil-bathed timing chain for maintenance-free operation.

Mercury's Optimax Two-Stroke Outboards

Mercury's Optimax engines also use sensors and a digital electronic control module (ECM) to obtain precise control of the combustion process. This process injects fuel under high pressure to get a stratified plume of tiny fuel droplets in the combustion chamber. The droplets allow an almost complete fuel burn, which minimizes exhaust pollutants. According to Mercury, the engines are about 45 percent more efficient than traditional outboards and exceed the EPA's 2006 guidelines.

The latest Mercury Optimax outboards use digital technology to allow the ECM to communicate with Mercury's SmartCraft system. The latter consists of sensors in major components of hull and machinery that feed information to a black box (the ECM) which then sends output readings to two or more screens. These readings include engine, boat, and environmental information along with engine monitoring and control.

Ficht Fuel Injection

Ficht fuel injection is slightly different from the foregoing methods in that Ficht engines use an electronically driven fuel injector controlled by a microprocessor to inject a plume of fuel into each cylinder up to 100 times per second and at pressures exceeding 250 psi. Because the engine ports are closed, the fuel burn is cleaner and more thorough, emissions are reduced by about 70 to 80 percent, and efficiency is increased by about 35 percent, according to OMC. Ficht engines have had problems with the injectors oiling up after prolonged low- and midspeed running, but in 2000 OMC was

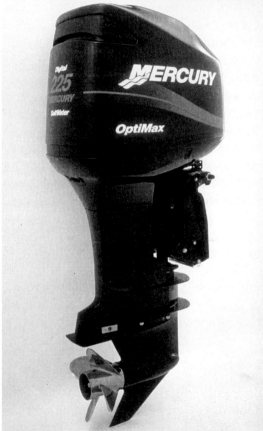

claiming that these problems had been fixed. As of early 2001, OMC went into bankruptcy, and its Evinrude and Johnson engine division was purchased by Bombardier. Bombardier has built a brand-new plant in Sturtevant, Wisconsin, and repositioned the engines in the marketplace. Evinrude will be the leading-edge engine with Ficht RAM injection, while Johnson will be the more conventional engine using a V-6 oil-injected engine. Evinrude engines are currently being produced from 75 to 250 hp, and Johnson engines from 25 to 175 hp.

CHOOSING AN OUTBOARD

What should you choose if you are going to buy a new outboard? There are a lot of good choices without a clear winner. I give a slight edge to four-stroke engines simply because they constitute a more tested response to the pollution controls being im-

Mercury's engines are differently tuned for freshwater and saltwater use. **Top:** The freshwater Optimax DFI runs at speed over a calm lake (note the transom cutout). **Above:** The 225 Digital Optimax for salt water. Optimax engines inject a stratified charge of fuel and air directly into the cylinder for efficient combustion. *(Mercury Marine)*

The power head of a Ficht fuel-injected engine, with injectors in the middle. *(Bombardier)*

plemented today. On the other hand, a four-stroke engine is heavier by about 10 to 20 percent.

According to some boatowners, a four-stroke engine is quieter, but Tim Banse, executive editor of *Southern Boating* and a factory-trained engine expert, says that some four-strokes only appear quieter because they make a more pleasant tone to the human ear. If you measure them with a decibel meter, you may learn that they are about the same.

INBOARD ENGINES

An inboard engine, of course, is inside the hull. This poses a problem in that the propeller must rotate outside the hull. Consequently, the propeller shaft is routed through the hull in a sealing device known variously as a *packing gland*, *stuffing box*, *stern seal*, *shaft log*, or *stern tube* (see page 104). Basically, these devices are all variations on the same theme.

The engine imparts its torque to the propeller shaft, but not directly. Since most engines run much faster than a propeller should rotate, there must be an intermediary between the engine crankshaft and the prop shaft to step down the engine's speed of rotation. This mechanism is the transmission, the gearing of which typically steps the engine speed down to around 2,000 rpm at the propeller. Transmission ratios are selected to match the engine rpm and the desired propeller rpm. The transmission also allows you to shift from ahead to neutral and astern.

Together, the engine, transmission, shaft, and propeller comprise the *power train*. In an inboard engine the entire power train,

except for the prop and part of the shaft, is inside the hull. Typically, the engine and propeller shaft angle downward a few degrees to allow the shaft to go through the hull, but the steeper the slope, the more inefficient the propeller thrust. Maximum slopes are considered to be about 15 degrees. Because a steeply sloped installation sometimes causes lubrication problems in the engine's forward cylinders, some newer installations have a transmission with bevel gears that allows the shaft to slope up to 10 degrees while the engine stays horizontal.

On some boats the engine is located well aft, and in order to get a shaft line as near horizontal as possible, the engine transmission drives a V-drive gearbox. This allows the transmission and shaft to be mounted ahead of the engine, with the V-drive near the middle of the boat. The V-drive torque is then diverted 180 degrees through bevel gears to turn the propeller shaft, which exits the hull in the normal fashion.

An inboard engine is oriented just as it is in most cars, with the cylinders vertical and the transmission attached to the back or front. A boat with an inboard engine driving a propeller requires a rudder for steering, and this is generally located in the wake of the propeller to increase its efficiency.

THE LATEST GASOLINE INBOARD ENGINES

It has long been said that gasoline engines are lighter and more powerful than diesel engines. Consequently, they are often used in high-performance craft. But gas engines tend to wear out faster than diesels, and new advances in diesel technology are making diesel engines lighter and more efficient. Electronic controls on larger en-

A Yanmar 6CX-ETE 420 hp inboard diesel engine uses sophisticated electronic controls. *(Yanmar Diesel America)*

gines make them more efficient and give better control over engine performance.

Gasoline inboard engines operate on the four-stroke cycle, as explained earlier, and have benefited from the constant refinements driven by the automobile industry. Electronic ignition and multivalve, multiport engines are now becoming common aboard gasoline-powered boats.

In spite of the advantages, however, many people do not want a gasoline engine in their boats because of the danger of the fuel vapor exploding. A gas engine installation requires bilge blowers and alarm systems that *must* be turned on before the engine can be fired up.

DIESEL INBOARD ENGINES

Because cylinder pressures are higher, diesel engines tend to be heavier and more strongly built than gasoline engines. They are also slightly less responsive, but their big advantage is that diesel fuel is not explosive at moderate temperatures: light diesel fuel has a flash point of 120°F (48.8°C), while gasoline has a flash point of about 80°F (26.6°C). Also important, diesel fuel economy is about double that of gasoline, which reduces operating costs and significantly extends range.

To increase their responsiveness, diesel engines are often *turbocharged*. A turbocharger uses exhaust gas to spin a turbine mounted on a shaft, which drives another turbine mounted on the same shaft to pump fresh air into the engine.

Turbocharging increases the mass of air in the cylinder, increases brake horsepower, decreases fuel consumption, and lowers the exhaust gas temperature. An internal combustion engine is, after all, an air pump. The more air flowing through an engine, the greater the horsepower produced. Turbochargers, however, work best when the engine is running at greater than half its maximum rated speed, at which point it produces enough exhaust gases to drive the turbine efficiently.

Aftercooling is another term you often see associated with diesel engines. As it is compressed by the turbocharger, incoming air is heated. Aftercooling cools the incoming air after the turbocharger and before the

Mercury's D7.3L D-Tronic diesel is another example of electronic technology in use on diesel engines as well as gas. *(Mercury Marine)*

combustion chamber to increase its density. This is because the denser the air is when jammed into the combustion chamber, the greater the horsepower produced.

The latest diesels are lighter, faster turning, and more likely to be turbocharged and aftercooled, and to have electronic monitoring systems for much higher performance. The result is an engine that is close to the same weight as a gasoline engine of equivalent power.

Gas or Diesel Inboard: Which One Is for You?

Despite the explosiveness of gasoline, gas engines offer advantages that for certain applications can outweigh the risks. For example, if you are looking for a high-performance boat, gas engines will give you more speed by allowing the boat to be lighter, everything else being equal. Gas engines are indeed still lighter than diesels, although the gap has narrowed—in other words, gas engines still maintain a higher power-to-weight ratio. The drawback to this point is that lighter gas engines are of-

ten highly stressed and may wear out more quickly than a heavier diesel engine if run at high speeds for prolonged periods. Gas engines also offer higher-rated engine speeds and a faster response over the entire range of speeds. In general, gas engines are less expensive than diesel engines and are easier to install and maintain.

Both engine types suffer from early degradation in the marine environment. What kills most marine engines, gas or diesel, is rusty cylinder walls and piston rings. The surprise is that this doesn't happen during the winter layup when the critical precision-machined surfaces are fogged with a sticky, protective oil. Instead, it happens when you are out on the water on a summer night, when moist night air condenses on the cylinder walls after running the engine all day.

Single or Twin Engines?

Should you have one or two engines on your boat? There are advantages and disadvantages to either choice. If a single engine gets a fuel blockage you will probably have to be towed home, but you may be able to limp home on one of two engines, assuming they're fed from separate fuel tanks and fuel lines. Investigate this when testing a new boat; some new boats cannot run on one engine. If you have just one tank, or twin tanks and a single fuel line, and if the cause of the malfunction is contaminated fuel (one of *the* leading engine problems), expect both engines to die when one does. In other words, true redundancy requires separate tanks, feed lines, filters, and controls for each engine. This is rarely done for recreational powerboats. Typically, only a rescue vessel or lifeboat such as those used by the Royal National Lifeboat Institution (RNLI) in England might have a truly redundant system. Still, unlike a single-engine boat, a twin-engine craft can limp home after losing or destroying a propeller.

There are boat-handling advantages to consider as well. A single inboard engine must use a rudder to control the direction of the boat, but in a twin-engine installation you can use the engines to turn the boat with or without rudders. With one engine geared ahead and the other astern, a boat can be turned in its own length. In a twin-engine installation the props typically turn in opposite directions—that is, the tops of both blades rotate inward. This balances the overall propeller torque, or the effect of pressure differentials between the top and bottom of each propeller. The unbalanced torque of a single propeller will tend to "walk the stern" and therefore turn the boat in one direction or another, a tendency that must be counteracted with the rudder at a cost of added hydrodynamic resistance.

A twin-engine installation, however, costs more (two engines instead of one),

uses more fuel, and requires more maintenance than does a single engine. You will also need more tankage and a larger engine compartment, and you will experience more noise and vibration from a twin installation. Although having two engines does not double your speed, it does give you some redundancy. Also, anglers might use both engines to get to the fishing grounds and then shut one down to troll at slow speeds.

One variant on a two-engine installation includes a large engine for higher speeds and a separate, smaller engine for low-speed operations. Electric trolling motors are usually fitted to fishing boats to

The Minn Kota Genesis trolling motor is used mainly for fishing but will get you home, albeit slowly, in a pinch. *(Minn Kota)*

power them at the slower speeds that trolling requires. Running a large engine at very slow speeds for a long period of time is not good for the engine, and a trolling motor lets you move slowly without worrying about your main engine. Trolling motors have a limited battery life, however, and are best on smaller boats such as bass boats, inshore fishing boats, and flat boats.

STERNDRIVE ENGINES

A sterndrive engine is a hybrid of inboard and outboard. (In fact these engines are sometimes called *inboard-outboards* or I/Os.) The engine is mounted inside the hull, but it butts up against the inboard face of the transom. The transmission gear goes through the transom and meshes with what looks like the lower unit of an outboard motor. The advantages of a sterndrive over an inboard are that the prop can be raised almost out of the water when not in use, and installation is slightly easier in that no rudder is required. A single hole must be cut in the transom for the drive and transmission, and the engine can be flanged to fit this hole, which must be carefully sealed. Sterndrives are slightly more complicated than straight inboards in that the outboard lower drive unit must be articulated to turn from side to side as well as tilt up. Turning in a horizontal arc enables steering to be done with the propeller. Tilting also allows a sterndrive to project the propeller thrust parallel to the water's surface for best efficiency.

Mercury Marine's 500 hp electronic fuel-injected (EFI) gasoline sterndrive. (Mercury Marine)

Mercury Marine's 350 Mag Horizon sterndrive shows how compact the engine and drive system can be. *(Mercury Marine)*

INBOARD, OUTBOARD, OR STERNDRIVE?

Which one is best for you? Again the answer depends on what you are going to do with the boat. If you intend to use your boat for water skiing, you would be better off not to have an outboard propeller sticking out behind the stern where it could injure a skier. Most ski-boats carry their props well under the boat, which makes inboard engines a natural choice. Anglers, too, benefit from an inboard engine: with the props well under the hull, there is less chance of fishing lines getting caught around the outboard or sterndrive prop.

If you do your own engine maintenance, you will find that access to an outboard is much easier than to an inboard. At the end of the boating season, you can simply unbolt the outboard from a small boat's transom and take it indoors to be worked on at your (or your mechanic's)

convenience. Changing the oil, filters, and plugs is much easier on an outboard because you have access all around the engine. Inboards are often hard to get at.

An outboard, however, will be noisier, more intrusive on deck space and activities such as fishing, and harder to work on when the boat is afloat. (If you work on an outboard when the boat is afloat, make sure all your tools are attached with lanyards to prevent them from dropping over the side.)

Sterndrive engines are easily worked on, but getting at the prop and the sterndrive unit usually means that the boat must be hauled. Because the engine is connected directly to the transmission through the transom, sterndrive engines must be located well aft, which poses a problem of weight distribution for the boat designer. Because of their complexity, sterndrives also seem to have more engineering problems than inboards or outboards.

JET DRIVE

A new form of propulsion, in a class by itself, is the jet drive. In this device, water is taken up into a tunnel in the hull and accelerated by a propeller in the tunnel. High-speed water is forced out through a nozzle astern. The nozzle is directionally controllable and also serves to steer the boat. If you want to go fast, by all means invest in a jet drive, but expect fuel costs to soar along with your speed. Also, figure on losing about 30 percent efficiency. In other words, a 70 hp propeller-driven outboard is equal to a 100 hp jet drive.

The advantage of a jet drive is that there is no propeller sticking out beneath the boat to foul on rocks or lobster pot warps, which means that jet drive boats are much safer when used in shallow water and around people in the water. Also, jet drives are installed in the transom, reducing the overall draft of the boat and making it easier to take into shallow water.

The major disadvantage of a jet drive is keeping the water intake grill clear of any fouling. Getting a piece of plastic or seaweed in the intake grill radically reduces the efficiency of the drive.

DRIVE TRAIN COMPONENTS

The drive or power train, as mentioned, includes the engine, the transmission, the propeller, propeller shaft, and bearings. Each part is critical to the success of the boat, and its function should be understood.

TRANSMISSION

If you accept for now (we get into more detail in the next chapter on propellers) that the most efficient propellers have a large diameter and are slow turning, and many modern boat engines are based on a marinized vehicle or truck engine intended to turn at high revolutions and have an instant response, you'll see that something must come between the engine and the prop to slow the latter down.

That something is the transmission. Basically it is a set of gears that allows the engine to drive the prop shaft ahead or astern. Note that the transmission of a boat is unlike the transmission of a car. Your car transmission changes through a number of gears, often automatically, and also provides reverse. On a boat the transmission need only go forward with one gear ratio and in reverse, which simplifies things a lot. Just as in a car, neutral is also required. (There are, however, a number of automatic two-speed gear applications being used. They are more fuel-efficient, make less smoke, provide a much shorter time to plane, and in many cases eliminate the need for trolling valves. Usually, the lower gear gets the boat moving faster than waiting for turbos to spool up before you get thrust.)

Transmissions are described by their gear ratio. On one side of the transmission is the engine, and on the other, the prop shaft. A typical transmission might have a 2.5 to 1 gear ratio, which means that an engine running at 2,500 rpm will drive the propeller shaft at 1,000 rpm. If we use a 4 to 1 transmission instead of the 2.5 to 1, the prop shaft speed would be 625 rpm.

The transmission ratio affects a number of things on a boat. The slower the propeller turns, the larger its diameter can be, which makes it more efficient. But fitting a 4-foot-diameter (1.2 m) prop on a 22-foot (6.7 m) boat would make the shaft angle very steep, which reduces the prop's efficiency. It would also make the boat very deep drafted and liable to prop damage, so a compromise is reached by selecting a transmission that steps the prop down just far enough to keep the shaft line fairly shallow yet still allow a reasonably sized prop.

PROPELLER SHAFT

The prop shaft is a crucial part of the drive train. Propeller shafts are used on all boats with inboard engines except those powered by sterndrives or jets, and they also appear on surface-piercing propeller-driven boats. (The blades of a surface-piercing prop are only half submerged at the bottom. This reduces the resistance of the propeller in the water and results in very high performance.)

The propeller shaft must be of sufficient diameter to prevent the engine torque from distorting it, and it needs bearing support to prevent it from whipping and vibrating. At the inboard end, a thrust bearing in the transmission transmits the propeller's thrust to the hull of the boat.

SHAFT LOGS

The prop shaft exits the hull through a watertight gland that allows the shaft to rotate. This gland is known as the *stuffing box*, *packing gland*, or *shaft log*. In most cases it is meant to leak slightly, and the leakage keeps the packing lubricated as the shaft turns in the shaft log.

A simple test will tell you if your stuffing box is working properly. After the prop shaft has run for a while, shut it down (loose clothing in contact with a whirring prop shaft is not a pretty thought) and then put your hand on the stuffing box. If the box is hot and you get burned, yell appropriately and then slightly loosen the bolts holding the packing in. A stuffing box should only get hot when it is being worn in with new packing. If it is a little warm, it's probably OK as long as only a drip or two is coming from the gland. If you have a lot of water coming in and you have tried tightening the seals to no avail, you need to get the gland repacked. This requires hauling the boat.

Dripless Packing Glands

A number of rotary seal packing glands on the market are dripless and are usually water lubricated with a rotary seal clamped to the shaft. The most common ones are Duramax, Lasdrop, and the PSS Shaftseal. They claim no wear on the shaft and are relatively simple to install, but the job should be done by a yard or qualified mechanic.

If you have a dripless packing gland on your boat, it should be checked regularly. Both ends of the rubber hose or boot should be secured by two stainless steel hose clamps. Check these carefully, since hose clamp failure will admit major amounts of water into the boat. Make sure you use stainless steel clamps and not clamps with stainless screws, which will corrode. Also, offset the clamp screws 180 degrees so they will hold the hose in place more firmly.

10

PROPELLERS

Yᴏᴜʀ ʙᴏᴀᴛ'ꜱ ᴘʀᴏᴘᴇʟʟᴇʀ is the output end of the drive system. To be efficient it must convert as much of the engine's power to thrust as possible. It does this by taking a bite out of the water in much the same manner as a screw biting into a piece of wood or a bolt winding into a nut. A propeller has several critical dimensions, the first of which is its *diameter*, simply the diameter of the circle described by the spinning blades in plan view. In general, the larger a prop's diameter, the more efficient it is, all other things being equal. *Pitch* is the distance a prop would move forward with each rotation were there no *slip*. For example, a prop with a 36-inch (91.4 cm) pitch will (in theory) move 36 inches forward each time it revolves. But because the propeller has an imperfect "grip" on the water, and tends to lose a little purchase as it rotates, the actual advance is less, typically by 25 percent or so for displacement powerboats and by 20 percent or less for planing boats. The difference between the pitch and the actual advance is known as the *slip*.

The efficiency of a propeller is based in part on the number and shape of its blades, the area of each blade, the prop's rake, the amount of boat hull or keel in front of the prop, the angle of the prop shaft from the horizontal, and other factors. In general, props with more blades vibrate less and allow higher loading per given diameter than those with fewer blades. They are also a lot more expensive and are more difficult for a propeller shop to fine-tune.

PROPELLER TERMINOLOGY

Blades Most boat propellers have three, four, or five blades. Larger boats may have six- to eight-blade props, but these are generally too expensive for small recreational craft. Generally, recreational boats use three-bladed props. Four-bladed props may cause a problem behind a centerline keel because the top and bottom blades are simultaneously shielded at the vertical, which can cause vibrations. When the propeller trails a substantial skeg or keel, it is better to mount a prop with an odd number of blades.

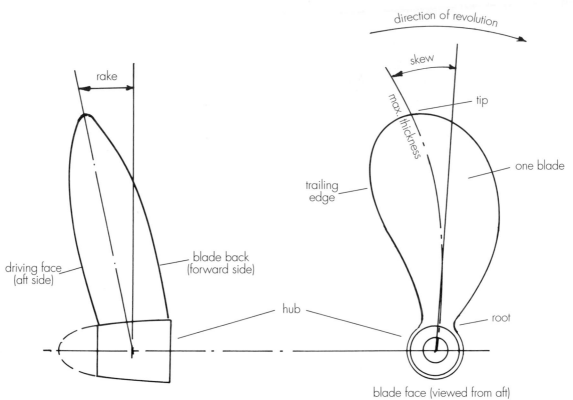

direction of revolution

rake

skew

max thickness

tip

one blade

driving face
(aft side)

blade back
(forward side)

trailing
edge

hub

root

blade face (viewed from aft)

Propeller anatomy.

Each blade has several parts: the *face*, which is the aft or high-pressure side (which may be flat or slightly cupped), the *back*, which is the forward or low-pressure side (which is slightly convex), the *tip* or outermost end of the blade, and the *root*, where the blade attaches to the *hub*. The front and back of a propeller blade can be thought of as a lifting surface just like an airplane wing or a sail. As it moves through the water it generates lift, which drives the propeller forward. Blade shapes vary, as the accompanying photos show.

Pitch Think of a screw turning into a piece of wood. If you turn the screw one complete rotation it will go into the wood a certain distance. In theory, props operate in a similar manner. (In fact this is an imprecise analogy—a propeller is more like a pump than a wood screw—but it remains useful for visualization.) Turn the prop one rotation and each blade will move forward a certain distance known as the *pitch*. In practice, however, because water does not offer the sure grip of a chunk of wood, the propeller advances less on each rotation than its grip would indicate. The difference between the theoretical and actual distances of advance is known as the *slip*, the amount of which varies according to load (think of a tug pulling a barge), to the speed at which the boat is moving, and other factors.

A typical round-bladed outboard prop. *(Mercury Marine)*

A five-bladed sterndrive cleaver for high-speed use. *(Hale Propeller)*

Hub Like the hub of a wheel, the propeller hub is its center. The shaft runs through the hub, and the prop is keyed to the shaft and held in place with a propeller nut.

Materials Most propellers attached to stainless steel shafts (for example, those used with an inboard engine) are made of bronze to minimize any galvanic action between the stainless steel and the propeller. Props for outboards are usually made of an aluminum alloy similar to an outboard en-gine's lower unit casing, again to minimize galvanic interactions. A few of the latest propellers feature high-impact plastic blades, and in some cases entire propellers are made of plastic. Ultra-high-performance props may be made of stainless steel or even titanium, but such props are extremely expensive.

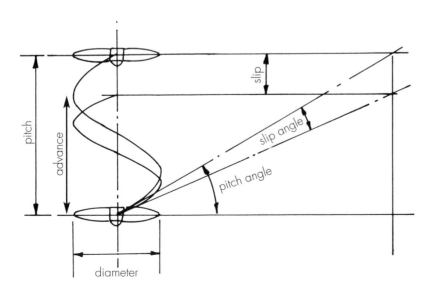

Slip is the difference between propeller pitch and the actual advance through the water of the propeller after one complete revolution. Face pitch is the distance the propeller would move through the water if there was no slip.

Rake *Rake* is the amount that the blade tip, when seen from the side, tilts backward from the hub.

Skew A skewed blade does not point outward radially from the hub. Rather, when viewed from astern or ahead, it can be seen to bend or curve at some distance from the hub.

Slip *Slip* is the difference between the theoretical and actual distances of advance by a propeller when rotated through one complete turn. It can be up to 30 percent or more of the propeller's pitch for a workboat or as low as 10 percent for a high-speed race boat.

Cupping A prop that is cupped has a slight rounding of the blade tip and the trailing edge. Cupping is intended to delay the onset of cavitation and reduce slip.

Cavitation As a propeller revolves, each blade develops lift in the manner of an airplane wing. When a blade revolves at high speed, an area of low pressure develops on its back surface (usually toward the tip), much like the incipient stall of an aircraft wing. At excessive speed or loading, the low-pressure area may spread across the entire blade, forming tiny bubbles of water vapor, and a consequent loss of thrust and onset of propeller vibration are experienced. This *cavitation* can be identified by inspecting the tips and trailing edges of propeller blades for the characteristic pitting that accompanies it. The small pits are caused by the collapse of the vapor bubbles with their attendant high shock pressures. Left unchecked, cavitation will eventually erode much of the blade surface and may eat right through it.

Torque and Side Thrust The rotational force applied to the propeller by the engine is *torque*. Torque varies directly with horsepower but inversely with propeller rpm, so a tugboat pushing a heavy load wants a big propeller turned slowly by a powerful engine. But an engine delivers more power at higher rpm, so we are confronted by objectives that appear mutually exclusive. Enter the transmission's reduction gearing, which enables the propeller shaft to turn at a fraction of engine speed.

A typical single-engine propeller is right-handed, meaning that it turns clockwise (viewed from astern) when pushing the boat ahead. For various reasons a prop blade gets a better grip on the water through the bottom half of its swing than the top half, and this causes a right-handed prop to want to "walk" the stern of the boat to starboard when the engine is in forward gear. This prop walking tendency is more pronounced in reverse, when it is not counteracted by prop wash over the rudder; in reverse, a right-handed prop will walk the stern to port. In a twin-engine installation with both propellers turning outward, the side thrust tendency is cancelled—another reason steering is easier in a twin-screw boat.

Volvo employs a method of eliminating propeller side thrust—which involves mounting two counter-rotating propellers on the same shaft. Each prop cancels the other's side thrust, with the additional benefit of 30 percent greater torque. With this setup a V-6 engine can move a boat as fast as a V-8, but with better fuel economy.

Handling is reputed to be better at a wide range of speeds and in reverse, making docking easy. Counter-rotating props, however, are much more expensive than a single conventional propeller.

Ventilation You may have heard your outboard engine racc as the prop comes near the surface of a wave. What often happens is that air is sucked down into the spinning blades, a phenomenon called *ventilation* that causes loss of thrust. Ventilation only happens when the prop blade is turning near the surface of the water and should not be confused with cavitation. Outboard motors have antiventilation plates to help prevent this, but these plates are sometimes mistakenly called *anticavitation plates*.

Variable Pitch Props On a variable pitch prop, the blades can be adjusted to change their angle of attack to the water. For high speed and low thrust the angle of attack may be very low, whereas for low speeds and high thrust the blades may be canted up to 40 degrees to the propeller centerline. On vessels such as tugs, which require high thrust to pull a barge or push a ship but also need to run at high speeds between towing jobs when less thrust is needed, variable pitch props are an elegant solution. Variable pitch props allow the prop blade to turn (or be manually adjusted) to change the pitch of the propeller.

Disc Area Ratio This is the ratio of the area of each propeller blade times the number of blades to the area of a circle the diameter of the propeller. It gives an indication of the amount of thrust available for a given propeller diameter.

INCREASING YOUR PROPELLER'S EFFICIENCY

A new boat is often fitted with props that have come directly from the manufacturer, selected to be as large as possible without interfering with the hull. (Typically, a minimum space of about 10 percent of the prop diameter is needed between the hull and the tip of the propeller blade for a displacement boat; for a high-speed planing craft the clearance should be 15 to 20 percent or more.)

Ideally, a boat's props should be "finetuned" to suit the boat's hull shape and displacement. A quick way to determine your prop's performance is to listen to your engine. If the engine cannot get to its maximum rpm, the prop may be over-pitched or oversized in terms of diameter or aggregate blade area—meaning that it is taking too big a bite of water every time it turns, and the engine cannot provide enough power to take that bite. It is like trying to start a stopped car using third gear.

If the engine reaches its maximum rpm easily (it may even over-rev), but the boat doesn't get to its maximum speed, the prop might either be too small or underpitched. Using the car analogy again, this is like driving down the highway in first gear. Other characteristics indicate other problems to an experienced prop mechanic. If you suspect your boat is not running at its optimum, have it checked out by an experienced prop shop. Select one that markets, repairs, and tunes propellers.

If you decide to get a new prop, first take a number of dimensions from the boat, starting with the distance from the shaft centerline to the hull bottom at the fore-and-aft center of the intended propeller location. This dimension tells the propeller expert the largest diameter prop that can be fitted to your boat. You'll also need to know the displacement of your boat and, ideally, its condition when the displacement is taken. For example, there could be 2,000 to 3,000 pounds (907–1,360 kg) difference in weight from the light-ship (with no fuel, no stores, and no crew) to the fully loaded condition of a 30-foot (9.1 m) powerboat. When optimizing your props, you need to know the weight in sailing condition, known as *half-load con-*

dition in naval architecture. In sailing condition, the tanks are half full, half of the stores are onboard, and all the crew is onboard.

A good prop mechanic will also ask a lot of questions about your boat's engine. What is the maximum rated horsepower? Do you have additional pumps and equipment running off the engine? In general, every pump or generator running off the engine absorbs between 3 and 5 horsepower; on such boats it is not unusual for the engine horsepower to drop by 10 percent between the crankshaft and propeller. In addition, the prop expert also will want

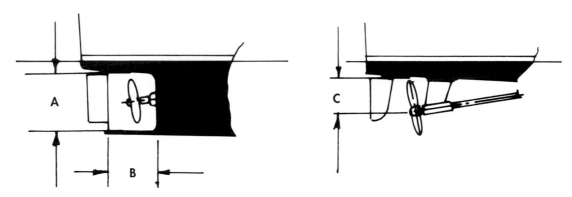

These are the parts of the hull you will need to size before buying a new propeller. **A** is the clearance between the hull and the bottom of the enclosure and **B** is the length of the enclosure. **C** is the distance from the hull to the center of the prop shaft.

These are the parts of the propeller shaft you will be asked about if you decide to buy a new prop. **A** is the shaft diameter, **B** the length of the taper, **C** the diameter of the propeller nut, **D** the width of the keyway, and **E** the length of the keyway.

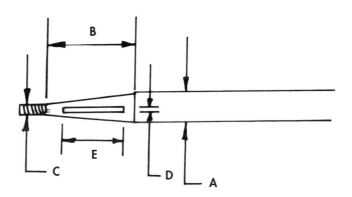

to know the maximum speed (rpm) of your engine, the reduction gear ratio, the diameter of your prop shaft, and whether the prop is to run clockwise or counter-clockwise.

All these data are fed into a computer program so that the shop can give the customer a prop that is within 98 percent of the optimum every time. If the shop gets inaccurate data, the prop specifications can be wrong.

When a prop comes from the manufacturer, it is pitched reasonably accurately but not fine-tuned, unless it comes from a company such as Rolla, in Italy, that makes top-of-the-line props. The fine-tuning is done by the prop shop along with any additional needed work such as cupping and balancing. Then the prop goes through a number of checks and measurements before it is delivered to the customer. This approach is typical of most propeller dealers and manufacturers who want to make sure that you get the right prop for your boat.

With recent technology, propeller blades can be measured by highly accurate systems that sense if a prop blade is 1,000 inch (0.025 mm) out of true. This information is fed into a computer and analyzed. For example, the Measurement Recording Instrument (MRI) system developed in the United States and available from Hale Propeller in Essex, Connecticut, www.halepropeller.com, can take thousands of measurements at each 5 percent radius (35, 40, 45, to 100 percent) to make a picture of the shape of the blade. Each blade is compared on the computer and optimized for best pitch, rake, shape, and other details. The system can also compare the propeller to the manufacturer's specifi-

cations, or it can optimize the propeller shape to suit the boat's power train. Major propeller manufacturers, such as Michigan Wheel, Federal, and many professional propeller shops use MRI systems.

COMMON ENGINE SOLUTIONS

You can get vibration, noise, and other horrible problems from your engine if you do not maintain it properly. Some problems, such as noise, are relatively minor and can be fixed at any time. Other problems should be fixed at once. In this section we look at some of the things you need to know to keep your engine in good shape.

VIBRATION

Kerthunk! Kerthunk! Kerthunk! You hear it as soon as you put your engine in gear. What's wrong? you ask. The fact that you only hear the sound when your engine is in gear tells you that the noise is probably coming from the propeller. If you increase rpm, the noise seems to quiet down but vibration increases.

A check of the prop may reveal that you have damaged a blade and that it is causing a lot of noise and vibration. The solution is to get the prop rebalanced and set up properly. Props can cause vibration and noise in more than one way, but quite often it is the vibration you will feel first. The cause might be that the blade is running behind a skeg or a centerline keel, or perhaps the prop is slightly out of pitch, or one blade is raked differently from the others, or the propeller is cavitating. Wear in the shaft bearings or whip in the shaft caused by bearings spaced too far apart also can cause vibrations. Each vibration has a characteristic pattern that can enable an experienced user to determine its cause.

For example, suppose the vibration is from the back of the boat. This is typically caused by the prop. But if the vibration happens when the prop is at rest, it could be the engine or transmission. If the engine is put into gear and the vibration appears, check the transmission. If the vibration worsens as rpm are increased, check the prop.

If the noise comes from the front of the boat, check for loose gear to see that an anchor or other gear is not lying against the hull. Quite often the hull itself acts as a sounding box that increases the noise of vibrations from the forward part of the hull. It may also resonate on its own if it is not lined with a soft, carpetlike material. If the vibration comes from the middle of the hull, check for loose gear but also check pumps, refrigerator compressors, and other mechanical devices. Careful sleuthing is the best way to locate vibrations. Then you need to figure out how to get rid of them. Like hull noises, hull vibrations often can be masked or eliminated by carpeting or soft carpetlike linings.

NOISE

"What's that you say? You got two nuts in the dark?"

"No, I got a tuna and two shark."

"Wassat? A donut in the park?"

Sound familiar? You've been on your boat all day and now you are having a hard time hearing because the engine noise is so loud. Engines are noisy, and without good sound insulation you can suffer long-term hearing loss.

Once while out fishing with a friend, I took along a decibel meter to see just how loud the engines actually were. At the helm station the readings were in the 90s, which is equivalent to the roar of heavy city traffic. The accompanying diagram shows the graph of rpm versus decibel levels that I developed for this 26-foot (7.9 m) boat. I have made similar graphs for other boats. All show high levels of noise at speed.

Decibel readings of 120 are equivalent to a jet airplane taking off. Decibel readings of more than 90 eventually can result in hearing loss after repeated exposure. Very high sound levels actually damage nerves between the basilar membrane in the inner ear and the brain, making this hearing loss permanent.

There are two basic types of noise: noise that comes from the structure in the form of vibrations, and airborne noise that comes directly to the ear. In a typical engine installation, vibrations from the engine can be transmitted throughout the boat. The way to cut down on this noise is to mount the engine on resilient or flexible mountings that absorb the vibration. The engine will also need to have intake lines and exhaust lines mounted to reduce the onward transmission of vibration. In submarines, for example, where noise transmission must be reduced to a minimum in order to avoid detection, the entire engine, generator, and motor mountings are placed on a raft that is totally insulated from the hull.

To cut down on airborne noise, you need to reduce the places where the noise can escape and where it can be reflected.

Unfortunately, from a noise standpoint, diesel engines need air to operate, which means that large vents are needed to allow air to get into the engine compartment. (One of the problems with today's boats is that the engines require a lot of air, and to cut down on noise levels many boatbuilders reduce the apertures through which air gets to the engine. The result is underperforming engines.) A typical 400 hp diesel engine may require a vent opening of about 24 square inches (15,480 mm^2)—say, 10 by 2.4 inches (254 by 61 mm)—to admit air, and another equally large to exhaust air. For twin engines, you would need twice that area. Noise escapes through these openings, but you cannot close them off. The engines won't run properly. The designer, however, can locate the vents so that the least noise escapes to annoy the crew. For example, they can be sited outboard and away from the people onboard, or high on the superstructure and out of direct line to the listener's ears. Or a forced-air fan can be used to increase the amount of air reaching the engine compartment, permitting the openings to be smaller.

In the steering area you may find that noise levels are higher because hard fiberglass surfaces reflect noise, in effect concentrating it around the person at the helm. One way to reduce noise in this area is to coat surfaces with softer fabrics, such

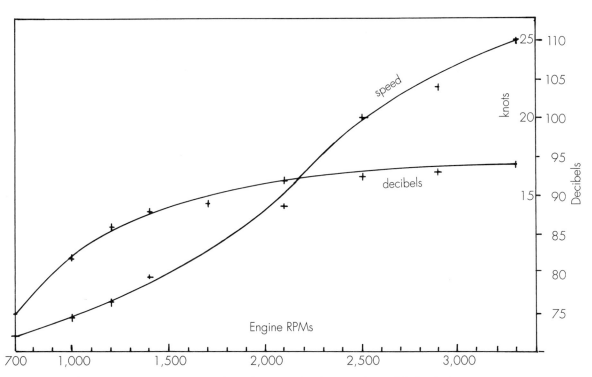

Engine revolutions versus noise. Notice how the noise level stays above 90 decibels when the boat is on plane. This can cause hearing loss over the long term.

as carpet or foam, which absorb noise rather than reflect it.

How can you cut down on noise levels aboard your boat? Joe Smullins, president of Soundown Inc. in Marblehead, Massachusetts, says that there are a number of things you can do. First, assess where the sound is coming from. You can use your ears or go to RadioShack and get a decibel meter (they cost between $35 and $50). Check to see if the sound is coming from the engine box. If it is general noise around the box, you may need to increase the insulation. If noise is coming from cracks around the engine box, put duct tape over each crack and check the sound level. Make sure that the engine is not being vented through cracks around the engine compartment. Smullins says that if it seems the noise level is still high after you have taped all cracks, peel the tape off and notice the difference. If you have an appreciable noise level difference, you will need to gasket the engine box. Any vents to and from the engine box should be well away from the occupants to keep noise levels down. If the noise is coming over the transom, look at the exhaust system. If it is noisy, you may have to invest in something like Soundown's Waterdrop muffler to reduce exhaust noise. Usually you can expect a 10 to 20 decibel decrease in exhaust noise with a water-muted muffler.

If the noise is loud inside your boat, you can install an acoustic liner behind the overhead or behind the ceiling. If engine noise is being transmitted through the cabin sole, install an acoustic carpet underlayment. Hough Acoustical Products makes something called the Carpet Pad, a mass-loaded vinyl bonded to a vibration damping foam intended to go under carpets.

If you have a high-performance boat, prop noise may transmit through the hull. In this case, you may need to install acoustic damping tiles on the inside of the hull. You should also make sure that your props are perfectly tuned to reduce both vibration and noise.

Selecting the right engine and propeller for your use, keeping the noise and vibration levels down, and keeping everything in tip-top shape are all part of the boating experience. The better you maintain your drive train, the more reliable it will be and the greater the resale value of your boat.

11

STEERING SYSTEMS

POWERBOAT STEERING systems tend to increase in complexity with boat size. The most common type on production power-boats is a wheel that translates its torque to the rudder either mechanically through a wire cable or hydraulically through a pump, hoses, and ram. Geared steering is often seen on smaller boats, and some very small boats are tiller steered. Boats with large out-board motors generally are steered by wheels attached to mechanical cables or hydraulic pumps that turn the motor, whereas small outboard-powered boats are steered simply by pushing or pulling the handle on the motor, which in turn uses prop thrust to change directions. Each system has its peculiarities.

The size and style of a boat's steering system depends on many factors: the size of the rudder(s), the speed at which the boat can move, the angle through which the rudder turns, the distance from the center of the rudder blade to the rudder-stock, the amount of feedback the helmsman senses, whether one or more helm stations are to be fitted, and even the type of engine drive system in the boat.

WHEEL STEERING

When you turn the wheel on a boat, do you know what happens between the wheel and the rudder? Many owners don't know whether the steering wheel turns a hydraulic pump or moves a stainless steel cable. They don't where the cables or wires run to get to the steering gear. If you don't know, go aboard your boat and find out now, while the boat is sitting at the dock. That way, you'll be better prepared should your steering fail at sea.

The most common powerboat steering system is the wheel, but there's a lot more to the system than just the wheel you put your hands on. The wheel is usually mounted on a bulkhead with the steering gear hidden behind furniture or trim. The wheel may be connected to a hydraulic pump, a push-pull or push-push cable system, or it may be connected to the rudder-stock by wires leading to a quadrant attached to the rudderpost. The beauty of wheel steering is that it can be placed almost anywhere on the boat, and you can have more than one. Most people know

The steering wheel controls the direction of the boat, but do you know what happens between the wheel and the rudder?

how to drive a car, so using a wheel to steer a boat is not difficult to learn.

HYDRAULIC

In hydraulic steering, as you turn the wheel, a pump moves hydraulic fluid from one side of the system to another. As the fluid moves, it exerts force on one end of the piston in a double-acting cylinder connected to the rudder or outboard motor, forcing the rudder (or outboard) to turn. When the helm station pump is turned back to the centerline, the fluid flows back to the other end of the cylinder, and the rudder returns to the centerline. Some systems use two single-acting cylinders to do the same job.

Some systems are said to have "no feedback." This means that a locking valve holds the rudder in position unless the helmsman turns the wheel. You still supply the effort to turn it, but the valve holds it in place until you turn it again.

Often the steering wheel activates a hydraulic pump that moves fluid through the hydraulic lines to operate a ram at the rudderstock. (Teleflex)

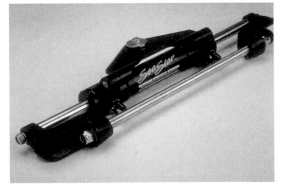

At the rudderstock, a hydraulic ram moves the steering arm and the rudder. (Teleflex)

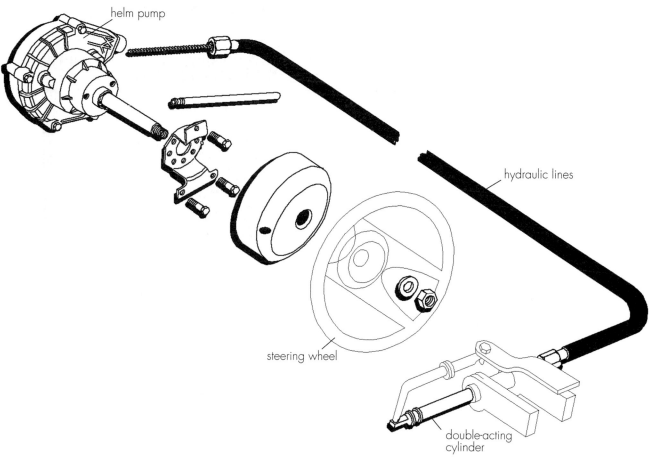

helm pump

hydraulic lines

steering wheel

double-acting
cylinder

Schematic diagram of the Teleflex MPS Hydraulic steering system. *(Teleflex)*

Should the system run low of hydraulic fluid, the operator can add more to a reservoir, which is often integrated with the pump. Should the rudder jam and the ram not be able to move it, a pressure-relief valve opens and fluid pressure is eased.

Adding other features is relatively easy with a hydraulic system. A second or third helm station can be dropped in at virtually any point in the line. An autopilot can be installed, as can cockpit steering controls. The number of turns from lock to lock can easily be changed, and maintenance is reasonably simple.

Hydraulic steering systems operate at a fairly high pressure, usually more than 500 psi (3,447,378 Pascal) for systems on smaller craft and more than 900 psi (6,205,281 Pascal) for larger systems. Consequently, high-pressure hose or copper tubing is required to keep the forces safely contained. Check with the manufacturer or a qualified service technician before replacing any hydraulic plumbing.

Cable

On smaller vessels, especially outboard-powered boats, steering is achieved with a cable system where an inner cable moves through a sleeve. These cables work just like the throttle cables on your lawn mower, in which the sleeve is held in place by a clamp on the motor so that the cable can slide back and forth inside as you push or pull a lever or handle. In a steering system, the inner cable is attached to a short arm either on the engine or on the rudderpost quadrant. This arm is so short you couldn't push or pull it by hand, but given the mechanical advantage of the steering wheel it becomes quite easy.

At the steering wheel end of the system is a long rack, either straight or curved, and a pinion gear (a cogged wheel). A straight rack is often used on smaller boats where space behind the steering dash is limited. A curved rack is used on larger boats. The rack is attached to a steering cable that runs through a flexible tube to the rudder or outboard. Turning the wheel moves the rack and consequently moves the rudder or outboard motor. Generally,

these systems have three or four turns from lock to lock. Some cable steering systems give some limited feedback to the helmsman, but most do not. Care must be taken to ensure that the clamps at both ends of the cable are tight and stay tight.

Wire

Wire steering provides a lot of feedback to the helm, and for that reason is not often used on larger powerboats. In this system, a sprocket is fitted on the other end of the steering wheel axle. Over this sprocket runs a chain, which is attached at either end to wires. The wires run via sheaves to a steering quadrant attached to the rudderpost. Turn the wheel to port and the chain moves over the top of the sprocket to port, pulling the starboard chain and wire to port. This has the effect of pulling the steering quadrant to starboard and causes the boat to turn to port.

With this system it is important to keep the wire taut (but not too tight) at all times, and to keep guards on all sheaves, so that if the wire stretches it cannot drop off the sheaves. Generally, wire steering systems are limited to about three or four turns from lock to lock.

The big disadvantage with wire steering systems is that it is difficult to locate the steering wheel a long distance from the rudder. This is because it's harder to route the wire fairly through the boat than it is to route a pull-pull cable or hydraulic hose. For example, if a boat has an aft cabin with steering from the bridge, the wires have to go around many sheaves or turning blocks to run fairly between the helm station and the rudderpost. This introduces a lot of friction into the system. Over long runs the

The Teleflex cable steering system wheel unit. (Teleflex)

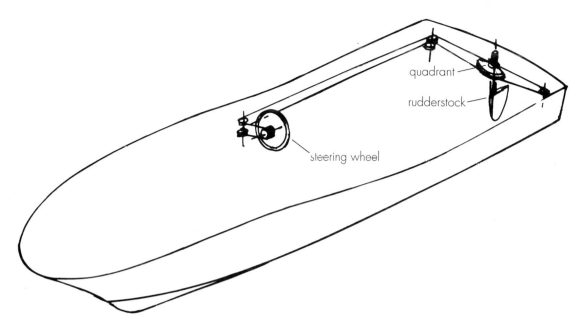

Wire steering is relatively simple, with a wire around a large drum behind the steering wheel. Rotating the steering wheel reels in the wire on one side and allows the wire on the other side to pay out. This turns the quadrant or steering arm mounted on the rudderstock.

wire can stretch if a lot of strain is put on it. When the wire is stretched on one side of the system it allows slack in the other side and the wire can drop off a sheave, causing a jam or steering failure.

There is a lot of feedback from the rudder to the helmsman, which is why wire steering systems are mostly found on sailboats and small powerboats. On a large powerboat it might require a very strong helmsman to hold the wheel against the feedback from the rudder.

OTHER TYPES OF STEERING SYSTEMS

Wheel steering is not the only system used on powerboats. Because other designs re-

quire the helmsman to be located near the rudder, however, they are usually only found on smaller boats.

STEERING WITH A WHIPSTAFF

Many yacht club launches and a few smaller boats are steered this way. A whipstaff is usually mounted on one side of the boat, although I have seen them where a wheel would normally be located. It usually has wires connecting it to the rudderstock quadrant. Push the whipstaff forward and the boat turns to the right, pull it aft and the boat turns left. (When the whipstaff is mounted in place of a wheel, pushing it to port turns the boat to port, pushing to starboard makes the boat turn to starboard.) This system is simple and

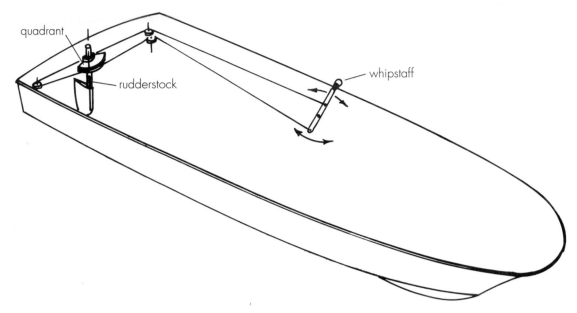

quadrant

rudderstock

whipstaff

Schematic of a whipstaff steering system as used on many harbor and yacht club launches.

easy to make. Its advantage is that it places the person at the helm near the boarding steps to enable him or her to help people aboard, get off the boat quickly to tie up, or cast off the boat and step right into the steering station. It also puts the person steering next to the dock when coming alongside. Its disadvantage is that it takes a little getting used to.

TILLER STEERING

On small boats such as launches, connecting a tiller to the rudder is easy. Using a tiller, however, locates the helmsman at the after end of the boat. A tiller is also very sensitive to propeller thrust that can exert a large force on the helm when the boat is turning at any speed. Consequently, tiller steering is rare on boats larger than 25 feet (7.6 m) or so.

RACK-AND-PINION STEERING

Rack-and-pinion steering works best when the steering wheel is located close to the rudderpost, which means the helmsman must be way aft. Consequently, this kind of steering is limited to smaller boats, where the person at the helm can see over the cargo or crew.

In rack-and-pinion steering, a cogged wheel on the end of the steering wheel shaft turns geared teeth on a large quadrant. The operation is simple and precise, with few parts to get broken or damaged. But it does have a few disadvantages, the biggest of which is that the cog teeth get worn. Over time, the middle third of the steering quadrant will get sloppy as the teeth wear out. Edson Corporation, which manufacturers many steering systems, recognizes this fact and offers a quadrant with a replaceable center third.

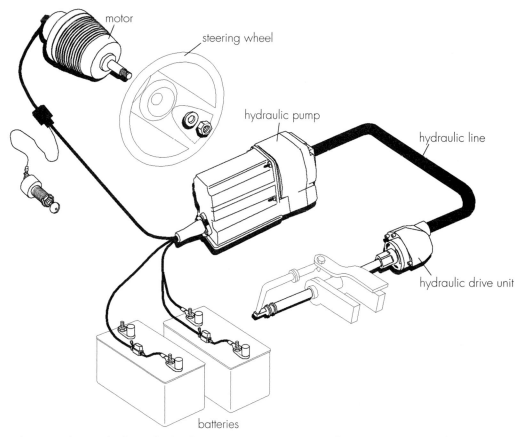

As this schematic shows, the latest hydraulic steering system uses an electric motor mounted on the steering column to send current to a hydraulic pump mounted near the rudder arm. The motor senses direction and magnitude of steering wheel rotation and sends a corresponding signal to the pump, which actuates the steering cylinder accordingly. *(Teleflex)*

Another characteristic of rack-and-pinion steering is that it has very little feedback. Rack-and-pinion steering systems generally have few turns from lock to lock. The number of turns is adjusted by changing the size of the cogged wheel on the end of the steering wheel axle.

RUDDERS

No matter what type of steering system is fitted, it is useless unless the rudders are properly located, sized, and turned through an appropriate arc. Rudder size depends mostly on the speed at which the boat can move. Large rudders are fitted to slower boats, and rudder size decreases as speed increases.

An efficient rudder operates just like an airplane's wing. It is a lifting surface, and turning it increases lift on one side, forcing the boat into a turn. To increase the effect of the lifting surface the rudder is usually located in the middle of the stream of water thrust aft from the propeller. This stream of water is accelerated by the prop; consequently, the rudder can be smaller than it would be if it were located outside the prop stream. A smaller rudder means less wetted surface and a slight increase in performance. The best rudder shapes are those that have the center of the rudder's area located slightly aft of the rudderpost, a design that makes the rudder want to return to the centerline. If the center of area is forward of the rudderpost, the rudder will want to turn to one side or the other, with a disastrous effect on steering. You have probably noticed this effect when your boat is going astern. If the center of area is too far aft of the rudderpost, on the other hand, it will take a lot of power to turn the rudder as water pressure will want to keep it going in a straight line.

You can have more than one rudder on a boat, and they don't need to be vertical. Some boats have twin or even triple rudders, although the latter are usually found only on larger craft.

If a boat has twin engines, it makes sense to have twin rudders, one behind each propeller, although some slower speed vessels have only one rudder between twin engines. Twin rudders are usually linked by a solid metal bar so that both turn together.

STEERING WITH TWIN ENGINES

If the rudders break off a boat with twin engines, you can still get home. It might be a little difficult, but you can steer quite well simply by increasing the rpm on the port engine to turn to starboard, or increasing rpm on the starboard engine to turn to

port. If you put the port engine astern and the starboard engine ahead, you can spin the boat in its own length. By careful maneuvering with both engines I have seen a skilled helmsman walk his boat about 10 feet (3 m) sideways into a dock.

BACKING DOWN

When backing down a single-screw boat with a right-handed propeller, you will find that the boat wants to turn to port. This is due to side thrust, as mentioned in chapter 10, and you will need to allow for this if you have a single prop. Ideally, your slip should allow you to berth portside to, so that the kick to port in reverse will bring the boat's stern right into the dock. The props on twin-screw boats usually rotate in opposite directions so that side thrust is negligible.

A boat's steering gear is one of the most important pieces of gear aboard a boat. Simply put, without it you can't get home. Understanding the steering gear on your boat, knowing how to maintain it, and how to operate it safely should be high on your list of priorities.

12

HOW A BOAT IS BUILT

FIBERGLASS BOATS ARE made from materials that sag and flop. A roll of woven fiberglass cloth is like a bed sheet in that it molds itself to the contours of the thing it covers. Just like maple syrup, polyester resin seeks the lowest point when it is poured. Unlike syrup, however, the resin sets up hard when a catalyst has been added to it.

Usually a piece of fiberglass cloth is cut to shape and laid in the mold. When it is in the correct place, the cloth is *wetted out*—that is, polyester, vinylester, or epoxy is poured over it and rolled until resin has completely permeated the fiberglass. Care must be taken not to roll too much or voids (bubbles in the fiberglass laminate) will occur. A high percentage of voids can lead to weak laminates and osmosis problems later in the boat's life.

THE MOLD

Because both the fiberglass and the resin mixture—called a *laminate*—need to lie over something to get their shape, production boats are built in a mold. Usually a production boat mold is female—the lam-inate is made inside it. Custom boats may be made inside a female mold or over a male mold. A mold is built from many layers of fiberglass over a wooden or foam *plug*.

MAKING THE PLUG

The first step in the building of a new boat is to make a *plug*. The plug for a production boat is an exact replica of a fiberglass hull, but it is built of wood or foam. To build it, a strongback is set up on the shop floor and sections taken from the hull drawing are set (usually upside down) on it. The sections may be covered with battens or strip planks or have a wooden laminate screwed and glued to them. A plug may take 6 to 8 weeks to complete using manual labor, and once the mold is made the plug is thrown away. Much of the labor is in polishing the plug to ensure the mold has no imperfections.

A new development in boatbuilding is the use of a five-axis computer numerical control (CNC) router that can cut a foam plug in a matter of days. Regardless of how the plug is made, the mold is built on it.

MAKING THE MOLD

The mold is made by laying a fiberglass laminate over the plug. This laminate is usually very heavy, much heavier than the laminate used in constructing the boat hull. To prevent distortion it is reinforced with wood or metal framing. (Alternatively, the mold for 172 ft./52.5 m naval minesweepers is made of stainless steel with steel structural reinforcing, at a cost of over $1 million.) The mold needs to be heavy because each hull laminated in the mold emits heat as it cures. This heat gradually breaks down the mold and makes it harder to get a good finish on the hull laminate.

After the mold has cured, the plug is stripped out and discarded. The mold's inner face is then polished carefully, because any imperfections will appear in each hull molded in it. Additional reinforcing may also be added. High-quality, well-maintained molds are essential to creating a good boat.

A similar procedure is used to develop a mold for the deck and for interior liners. Most boats require several molds. Typically, a production sportfishing boat might have a hull mold, a deck mold, an interior liner that incorporates all the furniture and bulkheads, a headliner that fits against the underside of the deck to give it a smooth surface, and other molds such as cockpit liners, shower pans, and toilet compartments. All these molds must be formed over wooden or foam plugs and can cost as much as a boat. Once complete, they are used to make the hull, decks and interior parts of each boat in the series. A mold can be used 80 to 100 times before the heat from curing resins deteriorates it so badly that a new one must be made.

LAYING UP A HULL

The first step in making a hull is to coat the inside of the mold with mold release wax, which allows the hull to come out of the mold (most of the time). On top of the wax comes the first (and ultimately the outside) layer of the hull, which is the gelcoat. As the outer surface, the gelcoat protects the hull and gives it color. It does not contain fiberglass; rather, it is a layer of resin about 20 to 30 mils (or thousandths of an inch/0.25–0.5 mm) thick. Gelcoats can be "soft" or "hard," but most are in between. A hard gelcoat will eventually craze as the hull flexes, whereas a soft gelcoat eventually goes chalky and needs refinishing. Boats built before the mid-1980s often

A new hull emerging from its mold. (Onne Van Der Wal, courtesy Little Harbor Yachts)

have a polyester gelcoat, but it has been found that moisture can penetrate a polyester gelcoat and cause osmosis or bubbles in the hull laminate. Today, most boatbuilders use a vinylester or epoxy resin gelcoat to prevent or at least minimize moisture penetration.

Over the gelcoat (inside it in the finished hull) is placed a layer of light fiberglass reinforcement, usually mat. If a heavy layer of woven roving were used, you might see "print through," the pattern of the underlying fiberglass material showing through the gelcoat. After the first layer, the laminate is rapidly built up, depending on the technique used to lay up the hull. Usually on smaller boats the entire laminate will be laid up in one shot and allowed to cure. While it is curing, its temperature is carefully monitored.

(continued on page 128)

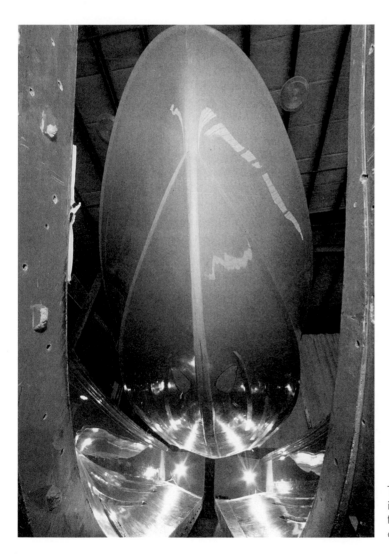

The Little Harbor WhisperJet 38 being taken out of its highly polished two-part mold. *(Onne Van Der Wal, courtesy Little Harbor Yachts)*

Reinforcements: The Fiber in Fiberglass and Other Composites

Boats are built with a number of reinforcing materials, and fiberglass construction involves a language of its own.

Glass fiber reinforcements are manufactured in many types and woven into many forms. E (electrical) grade is the most common glass type, while the most common fabrics are chopped-strand mat, cloth, and woven rovings.

Filaments are the single fibers of glass used in tows, yarns, and rovings.

Mat is a layer of short pieces of filament pointing in random directions. It is often used as a filler between heavy woven rovings.

A **tow** is a flat bundle of filaments generally held together with a sprayed-on glue.

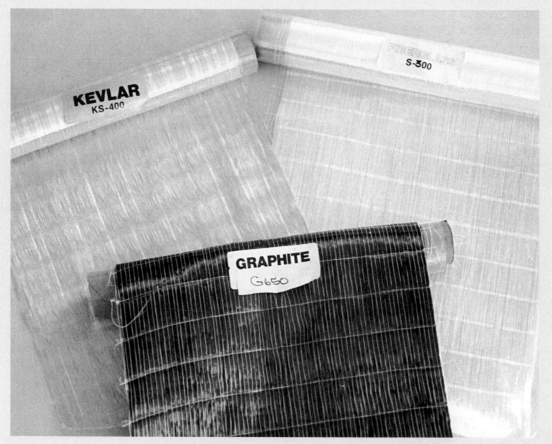

Clockwise from top left: Kevlar, S-glass, and graphite unidirectional nonwoven fabrics.

Cloth is a finish-quality fabric woven from filaments of fiberglass. The weight of the cloth is referred to in ounces—for example, 6-ounce cloth.

Woven roving is a coarser and heavier weave than cloth. Layers of woven roving build up laminate thickness and strength fast but are not appropriate for finish applications.

In a unidirectional **nonwoven fabric**, parallel fiberglass or carbon fiber filaments are stitched together with thread to make a sheet that is strong in the direction of the filaments and weakest at right angles to them. Such a fabric can be glued over another with filaments oriented at right angles to form a **biaxial fabric**, or a third layer can be added with fibers oriented along the bias to form a **triaxial fabric**. In areas of high stress, where the crimps in a woven fabric might straighten and elongate under load, a nonwoven stitched fabric may be the answer. A good source for fiberglass information is the SP Systems Web site, www.spsystems.com.

Fiber orientation is the direction of the fibers in a laminate relative to the centerline of the boat. Typically, fibers run at 0, 30, 45, 60, or 90 degrees to the centerline.

Biaxial fabrics are composed of two layers at 90 degrees to each other.

Triaxial fabrics are composed of three layers, usually at 0, 60, and 60 degrees to the centerline, but the angle of the layers may vary.

E-glass is the most basic material of the fiberglass family. It was originally developed as electrical insulation and was first used to build boats in the late 1950s and 1960s. Both its cost and its strength are quite low compared with the latest materials. It is still used by many production boatbuilders.

S-glass was developed to meet the requirements of aircraft builders, who demanded more strength and lighter weight. Because S glass is ultraexpensive, a slightly less expensive, high-strength version called S2-glass was developed for boatbuilders.

Graphite fiber, more commonly known as *carbon fiber,* is probably the best-known high-strength fiber. Originally developed for high-speed turbine blades, it is now common in high-performance boats. It is a high-strength, high-stiffness, lightweight material used to carry loads in areas of high stress where several layers of fiberglass would normally be required.

Kevlar is an aramid fiber made by Dupont. It is very strong in tension but not as strong as graphite or glass in compression. Typically, Kevlar is used on boat hulls to absorb impacts, in the same way that Kevlar bulletproof vests stop bullets.

A **prepreg** is a resin-impregnated cloth, mat, or filament that can be laid into a mold without adding additional resin or epoxy. After layup the laminate is cured by vacuum bagging with heat or autoclaving.

The **B-stage** is the second stage of curing a resin. As a thermosetting resin cures, it softens as it heats up and becomes slightly plastic. At this point it is called *B-stage*. Resins for prepregs are cured to B-stage and are then laid in the mold and postcured with additional heat.

THE LAMINATE

The laminate may be made up of several different materials. When fiberglass boats were first built, the almost universal standard was layers of fiberglass bonded with polyester resin, and most production boats are still made this way. The fiberglass may be E-glass or the higher strength S-glass, and it may be a mat or a square-weave cloth. In more modern fabrics, the filaments may be unidirectional—that is, all aligned in one direction and held together by a light scrim or glue backing—or they may be biaxial, triaxial, or even quadraxial.

More sophisticated laminates use carbon fiber materials in the same configurations as conventional fiberglass, and some laminates include Kevlar or other high-strength materials. The yacht designer determines what properties are most desirable in the laminate and selects the materials that best fulfill that purpose.

Fiberglass is applied in many different ways. One early production method was to use a chopper gun. A chopper gun has two outlets, one for fiberglass and the other for resin. A reel of fiberglass filaments is fed into the gun and chopped into short lengths about 1 to 3 inches (2.5–7.6 cm) long. These lengths are ejected from the gun into a spray of resin directed at the boat. Ideally, each length of fiberglass is coated with resin as it makes the trip from the gun to the mold. As long as the opera-

Laminating Methods

Autoclaving. After a high-performance boat part has been laid up, it might be cured in an autoclave, where both pressure and heat can be applied. The heat helps the resin cure, and the pressure forces out voids and VOCs (volatile organic compounds).

Hand layup. Most boats are built with each layer of fiberglass, prepreg, or other material being hand laid in a mold.

A **mandrel** is a male mold around which long, thin, carbon fiber parts such as prop shafts or masts are made.

Resin transfer molding is a relatively recent technique developed to reduce the amount of VOCs escaping into the air. The several methods available are collectively known by the acronym VARTM (vacuum-assisted resin transfer molding), the best-known one being SCRIMP, an acronym for

Seemann Composite Resin Infusion Molding Process. In all the techniques, the laminate is laid up dry and a clear polyethylene bag is placed over the mold containing the dry fiberglass laminate. A vacuum pressure of up to 60 psi (413,685 Pascal) is generated and the resin valves are opened. The resin is sucked into the dry laminate and is then cured under pressure.

In **vacuum bagging**, a laminate is wetted out, then cured under a plastic airtight cloth that is sucked tightly onto the laminate. The pressure exerted is not a total vacuum, but it is often several pounds per square inch. Vacuum bagging reduces the number of voids in the laminate and compacts it for better strength. The pressures achieved with vacuum bagging usually are not as high as those used in an autoclave.

tor keeps the gun moving this is a fast and easy way of making a fiberglass hull. If the operator pauses in one spot for a moment, however, fiberglass and resin pile up in that spot, giving an uneven laminate. The laminate not only varies in thickness, but it also might have voids where air bubbles are trapped. Voids, which may be up to 15 percent of the laminate in some cases, weaken the laminate and allow water to permeate into the open space. Another drawback of chopper gun laminating is that resin contains styrene and volatile organic compounds (VOCs), which are harmful to the environment, and spraying resin puts a lot of styrene and VOCs into the air. Consequently, very few boats, other than small dinghies, are built today using chopper guns.

The more conventional layup method is to place a layer of fiberglass fabric into a mold and *wet out* the fiberglass with resin. Here, the resin is poured onto the dry fiberglass and rolled with a metal or plastic roller until it has permeated the fiberglass fabric. Another layer is then laid over the wet fiberglass until the laminate reaches the required thickness. This method also releases large amounts of VOCs into the atmosphere. Though rolling the laminate introduces voids into the layup, this method reduces the number of voids to about 3 to 6 percent.

To eliminate some of the voids, builders may prewet the fiberglass laminate by putting it through a machine (called an *impregnator*) that soaks each roll of fiberglass with resin. The prewetted material is then laid into the mold. This method is also messy, releases a lot of VOCs, creates voids, and is laborious, so builders of higher performance boats may turn to

yet another technique using so-called *prepregs*.

Prepregs or previously impregnated fiberglass or carbon materials are fabrics wetted out with catalyzed resin but not allowed to begin curing until a later time. In the old days, prepregs had to be kept in a refrigerator until they were ready for use, because the curing mechanism was heat. Modern prepregs, however, can be stored at room temperatures because the final curing mechanism is an elevated temperature applied by a huge oven. A few companies are using ultraviolet rays to make the cure. Prepregs are expensive, however, and are not often used in production hulls.

Autoclaving is a curing method used when the very best part is required and cost is no object. After a high-performance boat part has been laid up, it is put in an oven where high temperature is applied to cure the laminate and pressure is used to compress the laminate. By exposing the laminate to pressure and heat, voids and VOCs are forced out of it. Of course, the shop must have a good ventilating system to extract and dispose of these VOCs.

A more common method used to improve the quality of conventional laminates is that of vacuum bagging the laminate. To vacuum bag, the laminate is laid up and wet out in the conventional manner and a cloth known as a Peel-Ply is laid over the laminate to prevent the plastic from sticking to the laminate and to absorb excess resin. A plastic bag is then laid over the entire mold and sealed at the edges. A vacuum of 6 to 8 psi (41,386–55,158 Pascal) is drawn, and the bag snuggles down over the laminate. Excess air and resin is pulled out of the laminate. Vacuum bagging reduces the number of voids to less than 2 percent and creates a much stronger laminate with a lower resin content.

The next stage beyond vacuum bagging is to use an even heavier plastic covering or a second mold that fits over the first mold (with room for the laminate), and draw a higher vacuum (in the order of 30–60 psi/206,842–413,685 Pascal). After the vacuum has been established, valves are opened and resin is drawn into the laminate. This method is known as vacuum-assisted resin transfer molding (VARTM, pronounced *vartim*) and goes under various trade names, such as SCRIMP. In general, VARTM moldings are only used when a high number of parts are to be made. A well-made VARTM molding has almost no voids. More on this below.

INTERIOR MOLDINGS

After the hull mold has been laminated, other components are laid up in separate molds. Depending on the performance requirements of the boat, these methods may be hand-laminated, vacuum-bagged, or VARTM. Most production boats are hand-laminated. When the mold has cured, foam or putty is troweled into frames, strakes, stringers or other parts to provide a flat surface to help bond the interior molding to the hull.

The largest of the interior molds is often called a pan. The pan typically has structural framing for the bottom of the boat, engine beds, bulkhead foundations, shower stalls, bunk flats, and flat surfaces to allow furniture to be bolted in. The bottom of a good interior pan will match the shape of the hull molding and will be carefully bonded to the hull to make a solid reinforced single-part hull.

VACUUM-ASSISTED RESIN TRANSFER MOLDING (VARTM)

The styrene and other volatile organic compounds (VOCs) emitted by most laminating procedures are a health hazard. State and federal regulations limiting the release of VOCs now make it virtually mandatory to do wet layups of fiberglass hulls indoors, with the air filtered before being exhausted from the building. Alternatively, a variety of closed-mold systems have been developed that capture VOCs during the curing process, greatly reducing the amount that escapes into the atmosphere untreated.

The method used by naval shipbuilders (building fiberglass minesweepers) and many of the larger fiberglass boatbuilders is known by the acronym VARTM—vacuum-assisted resin transfer molding.

On smaller recreational production boats you may see the trade name SCRIMP used to describe the construction process. The two methods—SCRIMP and VARTM—are almost identical. SCRIMP is an acronym for Seemann Composites Resin Infusion Molding Process after Seemann Composites in Mississippi, developers of the process.

The process is similar to vacuum bagging except that the fiberglass fabric is laid up in the mold dry. In a typical VARTM job the gelcoat is sprayed on the mold, and then the outer fiberglass layer, the core (if any) and the inner fiberglass layer are lightly glued against the gelcoat. (The method can be used for both cored and

A hull layup ready to be resin-infused. This boat is the Horizon 48 built in Taiwan. Horizon Yachts are available in the United States through Gilman Yachts, Ft. Lauderdale, Florida. (Jono Billings/SCRIMP)

noncored hulls.) The entire laminate, including frames and foundations, such as engine beds, is then covered with a layer of Peel-Ply and a special cloth with minute holes. Over all this is placed a vacuum bag (a heavy-duty plastic cover). A pump then sucks the air out, putting the entire layup in a 30 to 60 psi (206,842–413,685 Pascal) vacuum, depending on the part. Various hoses lead into the vacuum bag or top mold about 2 to 3 feet (0.6–0.9 m) apart, and each hose is clamped until it is needed. Note that the entire layup is still dry.

The resin is premixed and placed in buckets around the mold. When it is time to infuse the resin into the dry laminate, the hoses are simply dropped into the buckets of resin and the vacuum clamp on each hose is opened. The preaccelerated resin flows through the hose and into the layup under vacuum. The whole infusion process takes about half an hour to an hour, depending on the size of the boat. (In England, very large minesweepers are infused in less than an hour.)

The vacuum is held until the laminate cures, and then the vacuum bag, cloth, and Peel-Ply are simply pulled off the molded shape. That's it. No voids, no drips, no mess, and no unproductive tool cleanup time. In the shop, none of the laminators wear protective masks and coveralls. The job is much cleaner than the former messy, wet laminating approach.

In the conventional hand layup, all framing, engine foundations, and longitudinal structure must be added later. The securing of these components to the cured hull laminate is called secondary bonding and is not as strong as two joined parts that cure together. Secondary bonding needs to be done carefully or it may fracture, and the frames could pull away from the hull. Using VARTM, interior framing and supports can be installed in the hull dry and the entire framing structure–hull laminate infused with resin in one shot. This eliminates secondary bonds and makes the hull much stronger.

The VARTM process has been used to build some very large vessels with great success. In Savannah, Georgia, Intermarine SPA (now known as Intermarine Savannah) built eight 188-foot (57 m) minesweepers in a huge stainless steel mold. In Europe the same process is used to build 170-foot (52 m) minesweepers, with significant savings in labor and materials over hand-laminating systems. Another plus is the virtual elimination of lightweight cloths and mats. VARTM methods can use very thick fabrics, in some cases up to 120 ounces per square yard, although the more usual fabric is about 60 ounces.

Because the bagging and vacuum pressure are totally controlled during all phases of the process, the job can be repeated with an accuracy previously obtainable only with prepregs and vacuum bagging. According to the SCRIMP brochure, the navy has tested the VARTM method on laminates up to 6 inches (15 cm) thick and has found that voids cannot be detected using any of the current ASTM testing methods. (A hand laminate typically may have 8 to 10 percent voids, while a prepreg might have 2 percent voids.)

The SCRIMP brochure compares tensile and compressive strengths for VARTM, vacuum-bagged, and autoclaved laminates using a 140°F (60°C) postcure (many resins gain maximum cure and strength when subjected to temperatures above room temperature). Tensile and compressive strengths are similar for SCRIMP and autoclaved laminates, the brochure says, while strengths for vacuum-bagged laminates are slightly lower.

The VEC (Virtual Engineered Composites) method of construction developed by Genmar Holdings Inc. is similar to VARTM in that the fiberglass for the hull is laid up in the mold dry, along with urethane foam structural materials and reinforcements. But then a second mold is fitted over the structure and the entire hull—without any resin—is clamped down tightly. To equalize pressure, the entire mold floats in a tank of water while resin is injected under pressure into the totally closed mold. This keeps styrene emissions down to about 3 percent of open mold levels. Over five hundred variables are monitored by computer during the entire injection and curing process so that each hull comes out of the mold with the fiberglass laminate optimized for greatest strength. Thanks to the interior mold, the hull emerges with a glossy finish both inside and out, eliminating the need for an interior liner. This level of precision makes installing the remaining parts fast and easy, which also reduces manufacturing costs.

A hull after being molded using the VEC system. Note the inner mold elevated overhead. (Genmar Holdings Inc.)

EVOLUTION OF HULL MATERIALS

Not only have techniques changed over the years, but materials also have changed. At one time boats were exclusively made of E-glass, which is a fiberglass developed for electrical insulation. When a higher strength fiberglass was required, S-glass was developed, but S-glass was expensive so S2-glass was created. S2-glass became quite common, but has been supplanted in high-performance boats by carbon fiber. Today, most high-performance boats use carbon fiber, although a few experimental boats have tried a carbon fiber–Kevlar or carbon–S-glass composite.

Changing costs and technical advances drive the evolution of composites. Because resin is made from petroleum derivatives, its cost fluctuates along with the price of petroleum. Fiberglass also varies in price, and builders use more sophisticated laminates to reduce costs and improve performance. Biaxial and triaxial cloths have pretty much replaced chopped strand and woven rovings. Graphite and Kevlar cloths have become more common parts of a composite laminate. The number of cored hulls now greatly outnumbers those built with single-skin laminates. The state of the art for racing boat hulls has become graphite or carbon fiber with epoxy resin, while conventional boats still use fiberglass and vinylester or polyester. More esoteric boats might have a laminate of graphite, Kevlar and S-glass laminated using prepreg epoxy resins and autoclaved for full cure, minimum voids and optimum glass–resin ratios.

CORE MATERIALS

Many if not most boats built today have a lightweight balsa wood, PVC, or Core-Cell foam core. All this means is that the inner and outer skins of the hull laminate are separated by a core material, which stiffens the hull without increasing its weight. (In effect this is the I-beam principle.) A solid hull laminate of the same thickness would be incredibly heavy.

The most common core materials are closed-cell PVC (polyvinyl chloride) or SAN (styrene-acrylonitrile) foams and end-grain balsa wood. Both are fairly light. Balsa weighs around 2.2 pounds per cubic foot (35 kg/m^3), and foam cores weigh between 3 and 18 pounds per cubic foot (48 and 288 kg/m^3). In general, up to 6 pounds per cubic foot (95 kg/m^3) foam is used for boat hull core materials. Foam cores can be cut into almost any thickness up to 6 inches (15 cm), although few boats would need a core that thick.

High-performance boats may have a honeycomb core made of paper, plastic, or aluminum, although most builders of such boats use Hexcell, an aramid core shaped

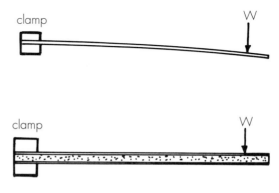

Comparative stiffness of a solid (top) and a cored (bottom) laminate.

like a honeycomb that is mostly air. This type of core requires vacuum bagging or autoclaving and is extremely expensive. Consequently, honeycomb cores are only used in ultra-high-performance boats.

RESINS

Recent years have marked important advances in resins. Polyester resin was the early choice of boatbuilders and remains reasonably inexpensive and satisfactory. But when osmosis turned up in boat hulls in the 1980s, production builders began to turn to vinylester or epoxy barrier coats. Osmosis occurs when water permeates the outer layer of a laminate and reacts with styrene in the laminate voids to form bubbles. The only way to treat a bubbled hull is to grind off the surface and recoat it with a vinylester- or epoxy-based resin. To avoid osmosis, builders use vinylester resin or epoxy resin on the outside of the laminate, and some high-performance builders now use vinylester or epoxy throughout the laminate.

Today's high-performance laminates may be laid up wet or with prepregs—that is, with fiberglass cloth that is preimpregnated with resin and only needs heating, photo-initiation, or some other catalyst to make it set. They may be laid up dry and then saturated with epoxy resin force-fed with a resin injection system, or they may be vacuum-bagged and autoclaved (heated and cooled under pressure). A boatbuilder may favor any of the above methods. For example, Barry Carroll, president of Carroll Marine in Bristol, Rhode Island, builds all his boats—power and sail—from high-strength epoxy with E- and S-glass, carbon, or Kevlar reinforcements. In fact, Carroll Marine is probably the leading

Core Materials

Core materials are used to increase the thickness between the skins (the strongest part) of the laminate. A cored laminate (sometimes called a sandwich panel) acts like an I beam, with the core absorbing very little load and the exterior laminates (or skin) acting like the beam flanges, increasing stiffness and strength.

End-grain balsa is one of the most popular core materials, especially for decks and cabintops. It is light, and it will not rot as long as it is totally encapsulated in the laminate. Wet or damp balsa, however, should be dried before it is laid up. If the laminate is cracked and water gets in, balsa may rot, but the rot does not often spread across the grain unless the leakage is severe.

Foam cores are available with varying degrees of density and flexibility. Most builders use Divinycell or Klegecell from Diab International Inc. of DeSoto, Texas, or Core-Cell from ATC Chemical Corporation in Buffalo, New York. Sharply curved laminates may use a scored foam core to allow the material to bend. Cored laminates are heavier if resin fills the voids between the core materials. A special filler is used for this purpose.

composite production boatbuilder in the United States. "We laminate all our hulls wet using our in-house impregnating machine," he says. "That way we control exactly how much epoxy is in the laminate. On our smaller boats the entire laminate is laid up wet-on-wet—that is, a wet or impregnated cloth is laid on another wet cloth—and postcured in our oven." According to Carroll, "We can get down to a 35 percent glass-epoxy ratio, but we don't need to. Our best composite laminate is B-staged prepreg cured in an autoclave using 100°F [37.7°C] postcure and four to six atmospheres, but nobody does it because it is extremely expensive, as you need a large autoclave to cure a full-sized boat hull. By using our in-house impregnator we can get a composite that is very close. We can also vary the thickness of our epoxy layer. For example, we usually make the outer layer thicker than inner layers for increased strength and abrasion protection. Inner layers have less resin and a higher resin-glass ratio."

Carroll adds, "At Carroll Marine we have never built a polyester boat. We started with vinylester and now use epoxies exclusively. I don't understand why some builders use carbon fiber in a polyester resin. That's like embedding a steel bar in sand rather than concrete. If you are going to use high-performance carbon fiber, you should use high-performance epoxies to get a high-performance composite."

Resins: The Matrix That Holds It All Together

When selecting a laminate, the core material and resin should be chosen to suit the intended purpose. If a brittle resin is used with a flexible core, failure could result if the laminate flexes too much.

Polyester laminates still figure large in the production boatbuilding industry, but the use of polyester has declined since osmotic blisters were found to be a problem on older boats. Since then (early 1980s) almost all builders use a vinylester or epoxy external barrier coat. Some use vinylester throughout the laminate, while others switch back to polyester after the barrier coat is in place. A polyester boatbuilding resin includes the catalyst and an accelerator—the latter being packaged with the resin and the former being added at the work site. When catalyst is added to the resin (at this stage both are about the consistency of maple syrup) some heat is given off and the mixture sets up into a solid lump. This is why it is known as a *thermosetting resin*.

Vinylester resin is a vinyl-based polyester with higher tensile and flexural properties and somewhat higher cost than ordinary polyester.

Epoxy laminating resins come in two parts—a hardener and the epoxy vehicle—and the two parts are mixed to start the curing reaction. Performance craft use epoxy resins almost exclusively, because they are stronger and stiffer when set and provide stronger bonds to other materials or previously cured resin.

PUTTING THE HULL TOGETHER

In composite boatbuilding, the hull is only part of the boat's total structure. The unreinforced hull is floppy when removed from the mold, and if not restrained it will flex and lose its shape. Consequently, before the hull is taken out of the mold, the interior structure is installed to give it rigidity. There are several ways of doing this.

PRODUCTION BOAT CONSTRUCTION

The hull liner or pan installed in most production boats is integral to a boat's strength and stiffness. Typically, a pan includes foam-filled stiffeners, a shower unit complete with showerhead and water closet (the head), bunk flats and faces, and grooves for plywood bulkheads. On some boats all the wiring and plumbing is installed on the pan before it is placed in the hull. Other builders install the engine on molded-in engine beds and almost completely wire the engine, generator, and batteries before the pan is dropped into the boat. While this makes the initial construction relatively easy, it often makes future repairs extremely difficult, because the pan may restrict access to parts of the interior.

The deck itself is laminated upside down in the deck mold in the same way that the hull is laminated, and usually stays in the mold to cure until the deck liner is ready. The deck liner often is fitted with wiring and sometimes the overhead lights before it is bonded to the underside of the deck. Because the wiring is encapsulated between the deck head and the deck liner it may be impossible to replace. Good builders solve this by installing conduit between the deck and liner to run cables in. Windlasses, stanchions, cleats, handrails and other deck gear may be fitted before the deck is installed.

The hull and deck finally meet near the end of the production line, when they are bonded with sealant and mechanically fastened together. Self-tapping screws are commonly used to locate and fasten parts in the hull-deck joint, but bolts with washers and nuts are better. High-quality boats often have the hull and deck bonded with layers of fiberglass as well as mechanical fasteners to ensure a good strong joint. Some builders, like TPI, now use space age adhesives in the hull-to-deck joint that are so strong that other means of securing the joint, including metal fasteners and fiberglass, are no longer necessary.

CUSTOM BOAT CONSTRUCTION

Custom boats are those built especially for one owner. Often the owner wants specific features that cannot be found in a production boat. The market for custom boats is small (estimated to be about 5 to 8 percent of the total boat market), and is mostly in the big-boat end of the market. Although some owners build their own boat to cut down on costs, most select a professional yard to do the work.

Unlike production boats, custom boats are usually built over a male mold that is later stripped out of the hull. Custom hulls can be built of many materials, including fiberglass, foam sandwich fiberglass, aluminum, steel, or encapsulated wood. The latter, often called *cold molding*,

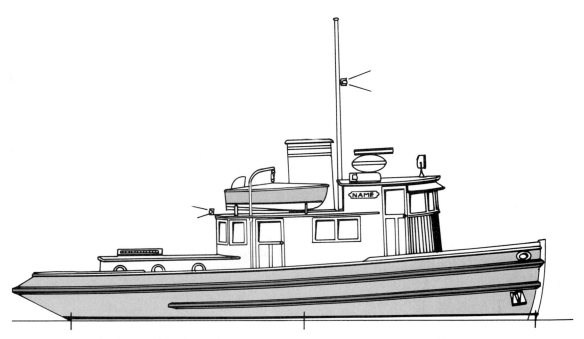

A custom tug yacht designed by the author.

was developed in part by the Gougeon Brothers of Bay City, Michigan, which also sells supplies such as the WEST System line of epoxy resins. WEST is an acronym for wood epoxy saturation technique. More likely, however, smaller custom boat hulls will be made of fiberglass, and the larger (over 80 ft./24.4 m) built of metal.

The mold for a fiberglass hull is usually made of wood. When the fiberglass hull has cured, it is taken off the mold and rolled over, then the interior structure (frames, longitudinals, engine beds, and any reinforcing) is glassed in place. When the structure has cured, the bulkheads are fitted and tabbed to the hull with thin strips of fiberglass.

After the boat's structure is in place the furniture is added. Often the furniture is made outside the hull and taken to the boat in large pieces, where it is dropped into place and screwed down. On smaller projects the furniture is built from scratch inside the hull; this is the most time-consuming method, however, because the wood must be carried to the boat, measured, cut (often off the boat), carried back aboard, and screwed or glued in place.

Once the furniture and large pieces of machinery have been installed, the deck is built on the hull (or it is built separately and lowered onto the hull). Then the deck is wired on the underside, deck gear bolted down on the upper side, and overhead interior liners added to hide bolts and wiring.

Custom boat construction is expensive (about 15 to 20 percent more than a similar sized production boat), but the owner can get exactly the boat he desires. First-time buyers, however, are well advised to buy a production boat and learn all there is to know before venturing into the world of custom boats. There is also something to be said for starting small and working your way up to a larger boat. Most people do not keep their first boat more than a year or two, because as they gain experience they develop a better idea of what they really want.

SEMICUSTOM BOATS

Semicustom boats use the same hull and often the same deck as a production boat, but are configured inside according to the owner's wishes. This has the advantages of keeping hull costs lower than for one-off custom boats (a custom hull is about 25 to 30 percent of the boat's total cost), and, because the hull design is tried and true, it saves the owner from having to make decisions regarding the optimum hull and deck shape. Quite often the cost of a semicustom boat is only a few percent more than a production boat.

SAFETY

Hull construction is more tedious than difficult, but it does expose builders to some nasty chemicals. If you intend to construct or make repairs to your boat, you will most likely have to work with fiberglass, resins, and topside paints. Carefully read the product information sheet that comes with the product (called a Material Safety Data Sheet—MSDS) and wear safety gear. In many cases, safety equipment may be as simple as a barrier cream applied to your hands to prevent contact with resins, but in other cases you may need a suit that covers you completely, a respirator, goggles, gloves, and even an air supply. Take the proper precautions when dealing with boatbuilding chemicals and paints.

A custom Pettegrow 36 sportfishing hull being built using Durakore, a balsa-plank construction technique developed by Baltek. The balsa will be fiberglassed inside and out, thus becoming the core in a sandwich construction. *(Baltek Corporation)*

Appendix

INFLATABLES

SHOULD YOU GET an inflatable? It depends on what you are going to do with it. The large rubberized tubes full of air that are the sides of the boat make great fenders if you have to pull alongside a larger yacht and are not too sure of your boat-handling skills. (After all a fender is an air-filled rubber tube.) But poor boat-handling skills are not the best reason for buying an inflatable.

Inflatables are rapidly gaining acceptance as a boat for all uses rather than just as a tender. Today RIBs (rigid inflatable boats—boats with an inflatable collar around the outside and a fiberglass bottom that gives stiffness and rigidity to the hull) from 12 to 18 feet (3.7–5.5 m) can be outfitted with consoles, seating and other gear, and are able to accommodate six to eight people in comfort. With the inflatable

A Zodiac RIB stowed on the upper deck of a boat. *(Zodiac of North America)*

tubes the boats have a reserve of buoyancy unmatched by any other type of boat. Because most inflatables have more than one tube, they have the capability of getting home even if one tube gets punctured.

With built-in gas tanks these RIBs have a 30- to 40-mile (48–64 km) range. Some of the inflatables on the market are fully tricked out with a cuddy cabin forward and can be used as a family sportboat, fishing boat, or ski boat, but are light enough to be taken to the water on a trailer and launched with minimal effort.

With an inflatable, you can carry a large number of people and maintain a high level of transverse stability.

In general, inflatables are lighter than conventional hulls of equivalent size, making them easier to drysail from a trailer. This helps reduce the cost of owning a boat and enables many owners to launch the boat when it is needed rather than paying for marina space. Having a big tubular life raft around the hull also gives many own-

ers an increased sense of security and enables them to enjoy their boat more.

PUNCTURE RESISTANCE

Can the tubes be punctured? Yes, they can, but only if the boat is mishandled. You can tear a tube if you hit a dock too hard or if the dock has protruding metalwork. You need to be aware that an inflatable is an air-filled rubber tube, and mishandling can destroy it. Having said that, inflatables are hard to tear. Even fishhooks seem to bounce off without snagging, and I know from experience that that includes a triple hook with an angry striped bass on the lure. I regularly use my inflatable for fishing and have yet to snag a hook. To further limit the possibility of punctures, it won't be long before Kevlar is incorporated into tubes, although Kevlar is a difficult material to work with.

This rigid-bottom inflatable clearly shows the fiberglass bottom. (Zodiac of North America)

RIGID-BOTTOM VERSUS SOFT-BOTTOM

Ideally, according to Bob Trout of Inflatable Xperts in Middletown, Rhode Island, every buyer of an inflatable should have a hard-bottomed boat. They require less power to push through the water, they are easier to tow and row, they get on a plane easier, and they usually have better engine supports and better bottom boards. According to Trout, the improvement in efficiency is on the order of 30 percent. Rigid-bottom inflatables, however, are more expensive and take up more room when stowed than a soft-bottom boat. Soft-bottom inflatables up to 12 feet (3.7 m) can be collapsed and stowed in the trunk of a large car.

Hard-bottom boats generally require a trailer, although the smaller ones can be collapsed and placed in a station wagon or on the roof of a car. A 12-foot-long (3.7 m) hard-bottom Zodiac inflatable with motor weighs about 200 pounds (90 kg) and can be towed by most family cars, with a tongue load of about 50 pounds (23 kg). A boat this size can be launched by one to three people without backing the trailer into the water. Although a hard-bottom inflatable is more awkward to handle than a soft-bottom boat, it does not usually weigh a great deal more—perhaps 25 to 75 pounds (11–34 kg) more for a 12-foot boat.

Inflatables are the vessel of choice for many people, from fishermen to divers, from families to intrepid voyagers. One inflatable has powered around the world using soybean oil instead of diesel. Others have traversed the open spaces of the Atlantic Ocean. No matter what your needs or the size of your budget, there is probably an inflatable for you.

You can use an inflatable as your primary boat. Here, twin engines power a large RIB. (AB Inflatables)

WHAT TO LOOK FOR: FEATURES AND CONSTRUCTION

Most inflatables are made two distinct ways, each according to the type of fabric used to form the tubes. The older of the two is Hypalon, a registered trade mark of Dupont; the newer is PVC (polyvinyl chloride).

Hypalon boats, such as Avon, Achilles, and larger Zodiacs, are constructed from individually hand-glued panels. The glue has to be applied, allowed to cure slightly, and then the seams are pressed together. Hypalon inflatables therefore, are labor intensive, which is why most inflatables are assembled in countries with low labor rates, such as Venezuela, Korea, and China. The seams on PVC boats, like those made by Zodiac and its other brands, are electronically welded. The welding machines are robotic, which reduces labor costs and results in slightly lower prices. PVC has less UV protection than Hypalon, which makes it a less desirable material for use in the tropics. PVC boats, however, stay inflated much longer than Hypalon boats. According to J. J. Marie, president of Zodiac North America, "You can expect to reinflate a Hypalon boat about once a week, older boats sometimes once a day, and a PVC boat about once a month."

Larger and high-speed inflatables almost exclusively use Hypalon bonded to a fiberglass or alloy bottom. Larger vessels also use the tubes as spray deflectors to keep water from coming inboard at high speeds as well as using them to gain some buoyancy when heading into large waves.

Selecting the right engine is of critical importance for powering an inflatable. This small inflatable is powered by a 5 hp Nissan engine. (Nissan Marine)

Index

Numbers in **bold** refer to pages with illustrations

A

active stabilizers, **74**–75
aftercooling, in diesel engines, 98–99
amas, 34, 35
anchor handling gear, 57, **58**
anchor storage, 85–86
antiroll tanks, 73–**74**
Aquasport 161 Tournament Cat, **35**
autoclaving, 128, 129

B

backing down, 122
ballast, and stability, 65
bass boats, **41**–42
beam, and stability, 65
berths, **79**, 82
biaxial fabric, 127
bilge keels, 23
bilge pumps, 83–84
block coefficient, 48
boatbuilding. *See also* fiberglass; resins
    autoclaving, 128, 129
    cold molding, 136–37
    core materials, **133**–34
    gelcoat, 124–25
    hull construction, 124–25, 128–30, 136–**38**
    interior molds, 130
    laminating methods, 128
    layup method, 128–30
    materials, **126**–30, 133–35
    mold, 123–**24**, **125**
    plug, 123
    SCRIMP method, 128, 130, 132
    vacuum bagging, 128, 129
    VARTM method, 128, 130–32, **131**
    Virtual Engineered Composites (VEC), **132**
boat evaluation tools, 47–49
boat handling, and engine configuration, 100
Boston Whaler, **20**
bow shape, 52, **54**, 55
    bulbous, 28–**29**
    deep-V hulls, 37
    round-bilged hull, 28–29
    semidisplacement hulls, 44
    V-hull boats, **14**–**15**, 31–**32**
bridge design, **80**, 81–82
bulbous bow, 28–**29**
bunks, **79**, 82
buttock lines, 13, **18**
    V-hull boats, **14**–**15**

C

cabin design, **80**
    catamarans, 35
    comfort and, **79**–81
    head and shower compartment, 82
    lighting, 77–78
    seaworthiness and, 69–70
    sleeping quarters, 82
    storage, 84–85
    V-hull boats, 33
cabin sole, storage under, 85
cable steering systems, **118**
Callan 55, **39**
canoe-stern cruising hull, **27**
    freeboard, 30–31
    stability, 27, **62**
capacity, of boat, 46
carbon fiber, 127

carburetors, 92–93
Carroll Marine, 134–35
catamarans, 3, **35**. *See also* slim hulls
    cabin design, 35
    fuel efficiency, 35
    stability, **62**
cathedral hull, **20**
cavitation, 108
center of buoyancy, **62**, **65**
center of gravity, 60–**67**
chine flat, **14**, 64
chines, **19–20**
    configuration comparisons, 45–46
    stability, 64
    V-hull boats, **14–15**, 31–**33**
chopper gun, 128–29
Cigarette Café 33 Open, **37**
Clerk, Dugald, 88
cloth, for fiberglassing, 127
cold molding, 136–37
comfort
    bridge design, 81–82
    cabin design, **79**–81, 82
    cockpit, 77
    deck design, 75–76
    hull shapes and, 11, 72–73
    lighting, 77–78
    location on boat and, 73
    speed and, 10–11, 72–73
    trade-off with speed and range, 3
composite boatbuilding materials, **126**–27, 133
computer software, for hull design, 18–19
core materials, **133**–34
cost, of boat, 11–12
    construction methods and, 136–38
    cubic number for comparison, 48
cubic number (CN), 48
custom boat construction, 136–**38**

D
deadrise, 20–**21**
    angle in planing hulls, 36
    bass boats, 42
    deep-V hulls, 37
    offshore sportfishing boats, 42
    saltwater flats boats, 40
    V-hull boats, **14–15**, 31
decibel meter, 112, 114
deck design
    safety and, 75–76, 77
    seaworthiness, 70–71
deck gear, 57–58. *See also specific gear*
deck lighting, 78
deep-V hulls, **2**. *See also* V-hull boats

bow shape, 37
    deadrise, 20–**21**, 37
    longitudinal center of gravity (LCG), 39
    midbody, 37
    prismatic coefficient, 48–49
    sheerline, **39**
    stern, 39
    strake placement, **38**, **39**
    strakes, 37
destroyer stern, 36
Diesel, Rudolph, 88
diesel direct injection, 93
diesel engines, 91
    aftercooling, 98–99
    compared to gasoline, 99
    diesel direct injection, 93
    inboard, **98–99**
    noise and, 113
    turbocharger, 98, 99
    Yanmar 6C-ETE 420 hp, **98**
direct fuel injection, 93
displacement hulls, about, 2–3, 26
    prismatic coefficient, 48–49
    speed and, 4–6
displacement hulls, types of
    catamarans, **35**
    round-bilge trawlers, **27**–31
    skinny boats, 34
    trawler yachts, 26–27
    V-hull cruisers, 31–34, **32**, **33**
displacement–length ratio (D/L), 47
doors, 81
dripless packing glands, 104
drive train. *See* power train
durability, of rigid inflatable boats (RIBs), 140
Durakore hull construction, **138**
dynamic stabilization in planing hulls, 75

E
E-glass, 127
electric boat speed record, 3
electric steering systems, **121**
electric trolling motors, **100**–101
electronic fuel injection (EFI), 93, 94–96
electronics storage, 84
end-grain balsa, 134
engine configuration, and boat handling, 100
engine emission standards, 92
engine placement, and weight, 33
engine room
    design for maintenance, 83
    lighting, 78
    seaworthiness, 70
    storage, 85

engines, about
 advantages by type, 102
 early, 87–88
 noise, 112–14, **113**
 single compared to twin, 99–101
 troubleshooting, 111–14
 vibration, 111–12
engines, types of
 diesel, 98–99
 four-stroke cycle, **90**, 92
 gasoline, 88–**90**
 inboard, 97–101
 inboard-outboard (I/O), **101**–2
 outboard, 91–97
 two-stroke cycle, 88–**89**
epoxy laminating resins, 135

F
fiberglass
 laminate, 123, 128–32
 prepreg cloth, 127, 129, 134
 types, **126**–27
Ficht fuel injection, 95–**96**
filaments, 126
fishing hulls, types of
 bass boats, **41**–42
 offshore sportfishing boats, **42**
 saltwater flats boats, **40**–41
flare, **22**, 23
 round-bilged hulls, 29
 V-hull boats, **14–15**, 31
flat-bottom hulls, 1–2
 chines, **19**
 deadrise, 20–**21**
flooding, and stability, 66–**67**
flopper stoppers, 75
flume tanks, 73–**74**
foam cores, 134
form stability, 60–**62**
four-stroke cycle engines, **90**, 92
 Suzuki 25 hp EFI, **95**
freeboard, 21–**22**, **51**
 round-bilge hulls, 30–31
 seaworthiness and, 6–7
free surface, 66–**67**
Froude, William, 4
Froude number and law, 4–5, 34, 47
fuel efficiency, 46
 catamarans, 35
 planing hulls, 44
 propeller side thrust and, 108
fuel injection
 diesel direct injection, 93
 direct fuel injection, 93

electronic, 93, 94–95
Ficht fuel injection, 95–**96**
high-pressure direct injection, 93–94
in outboard engines, 93

G
galley storage, 84
gasoline engines, 88–**90**
 compared to diesel, 99
 inboard, 97–98
 outboard, 91–97
gelcoat, 124–25
glass fiber reinforcements, 126
Gougeon Brothers, 137
graphite fiber, 127, 133
graphite unidirectional nonwoven fabric, **126**

H
half-load condition, 110
handholds, 76
hand layup, of hulls, 128
hard-chine hull, **19**
head and shower compartment, 82
heel angle, 34, 66
Hells Bay Whipray 16, **41**
helm station, **80**, 81
high-pressure direct injection (HPDI), 93–94
Honda 130 hp engine, **93**
Horizon 48, **131**
horsepower calculation, 48
HPDI, 93–94
hull construction, 124–25. *See also* boatbuilding
 custom boats, 136–**38**
 production boats, 136
 safety, 138
 semicustom boats, 138
hull design computer software, 18–19
hull design factors. *See also* hull shapes, about;
  hull shapes, types of
 comfort, 10–11
 cost, 11–12
 prismatic coefficient, 48–49
 range, 10
 seaworthiness, 6–9
 speed, 4–6
 stability, 59–67
hull design features. *See also* hull shapes about;
  hull shapes, types of
 bow shape, 52, **54**, 55
 chines, **19–20**
 deadrise, 20–**21**
 deck gear, 57–58

hull design features *(continued)*
    flare, 23
    freeboard, 21–**22**, **51**
    keels and bilge keels, **23**
    sheerline, 50–**52**, **53**
    stern shape, 55
    strakes, 23–**24**
    superstructure styling, **55**–57
    trim angle and trim tabs, **24**–**25**
hull evaluation tools, 47–49
hull shapes, about, 1–4
    comfort and, 11, 72–73
    questions about, 45–46
    seaworthiness and, 69
    seaworthiness factors by, 8–9
    stability and, **61**–**62**
hull shapes, types of
    displacement, 26–**35**
    fishing, **40**–**42**
    planing, **36**–**39**
    semiplaning, **43**–45
hull speed, 4–6
hump region, **5**–6
hydraulic steering systems, **116**–**17**, **121**
hydrodynamic lift, **36**
hydroplane-style hull, **1**–2

I
inboard engines, 97–101
    compared to outboards or sterndrives,
        102
    diesel, 91, **98**–**99**
    gasoline, 97–98
    gasoline compared to diesel, 99
    power train, 97
inboard-outboard (I/O) engines, **101**–2
inflatable boats. *See* rigid inflatable boats (RIBs)
internal combustion engines, 87

J
jet drive, 103

K
keel, **23**
    lines plan drawing, **16**–**17**
    propeller configuration and, 30
    round-bilge hull, **27**, 31
Kevlar, **126**, 127, 133

L
ladders, **76**–77
laminate, 123, 128–32

laminating methods, in boatbuilding, 128
length-to-beam ratio (L/B), 48, 61
Lenoire engines, 87–88
lighting
    cabin, 77–78
    deck, 78
    engine room, 78
    safety and, 77–78
lines plan drawings
    buttock lines, 13
    lobster-boat-style hull, **16**–**17**
    plan view, 13, 18
    profile view, 13
    sectional view, 18–19
    V-hull boat, **14**–**15**
Little Harbor WhisperJet 38, **125**
lobster-boat-style hulls, 27–28, 44
    chines, **19**
    keel, **23**
    lines plan drawing, **16**–**17**
location on boat, and comfort, 73
lockers, 84
longitudinal center of buoyancy (LCB), 33,
    62, 63, 73
longitudinal center of gravity (LCG), 33, 39,
    62, 63, 73
longitudinal stability, 60, 64, 65
Luhrs 290, **22**
Luhrs 400 Open, **3**

M
maintenance, 83–84
mandrel, 128
mat, 126
Measurement Recording Instrument (MRI),
    111
Mercury D7.3L D-Tronic diesel engine, **99**
Mercury Marine 500 hp EFI sterndrive,
    101
Mercury Marine 350 Mag Horizon sterndrive,
    102
Mercury Optimax engine, 95, **96**
metacenter (M), 60, **65**
metacentric height (GM), **65**, 66–**67**
Minn Kota Genesis trolling motor, **100**
Minn Kota trolling motor, **41**
Miss Budweiser, **1**, **2**, 64
moderate-displacement hull, 2–3
molds, for boatbuilding, 123–**24**, 130

N
N. A. Otto Company, 87–88
navigation table, 81–82

noise
    from engines, **113**
    identification and repair, 112–14
Nordhavn trawler yacht, **4**

O

offshore sportfishing boats, 42
operating expenses, 12
Otto, *see* N. A. Otto Company
outboard engines, 91–97, **93**
    compared to inboards or sterndrives, 102
    comparison of types, 96–97
    Ficht fuel injection, 95–**96**
    fuel injection, 93
outboard-powered boat speed record, 3
outriggers, 34, 35
overhead storage, 85

P

packing glands, 97, 104
packing glands, dripless, 104
paravanes, 75
passageways, 81
passive stabilizers, 73–**74**
Pettegrow 36 sportfishing hull, **138**
planing hulls, about
    buttock lines, **18**
    deadrise angle, 36
    dynamic stabilization, 75
    fuel efficiency, 44
    lifting strakes, 36
    sheerline, 36–37
    speed and, 4–6
    stern shape, 36
    strakes, 23–**24**
planing hulls, types of
    high-speed deep-V, 37, **38**, 39
    ski boats, **38**
    stepped, 39
plan view of lines plan, 13, 18
    lobster-boat-style hull, **16–17**
    V-hull boat, **14–15**
plug, 123
polyester laminate, 135
power cruiser, **32**
power-to-weight ratio, 48
power train
    components, 103–4
    in inboard engines, 97
    packing glands, 97, 104
    propellers, 105–11
    propeller shaft, 97, 104
    shaft logs, 97, 104

stuffing box, 97, 104
    transmission, 103–4
prepreg cloth, 127, 129, 134
prismatic coefficient, 48–49
Pro Air Nautique wakeboarding boat, **6**
production boat construction, 136
profile view of lines plan, 13, **51**
    lobster-boat-style hull, **16–17**
    V-hull boat, **14–15**
propellers, about, **106**
    blades, 105–**6**
    cavitation, 108
    configuration with keels, 30
    cupping, 108
    diameter, 105
    disc area ratio, 109
    efficiency, 109–12, 114
    grip, 105
    hub, 107
    materials, 107
    pitch, 105, 106, **107**, 111
    placement with inboard engine, 97
    prop replacement, 109–11, **110**
    rake, 108
    shaft, 97, 104
    side thrust, 108–9
    skew, 108
    slip, 105, 106, **107**, 108
    torque, 100, 108–9
    ventilation, 109
    walk the stern, 100, 108
propellers, types of
    outboard prop, round-bladed, **107**
    sterndrive cleaver, five-bladed, **107**
    variable pitch, 109

R

rack-and-pinion steering systems, 120–21
radar arches, 58
range
    factors that affect, 10
    formula, 46
    rigid inflatable boats (RIBs), 140
    trade-off with speed and comfort, 3
refrigerator storage, 84–85
resins, 134–35
    B-stage, 127
    epoxy, 135
    laminate, 123, 128–32
    polyester, 135
    vinylester, 135
    WEST System, 137
resin transfer molding, 128
restoring moment, 63–64, **65**

reverse chines, **20**
reverse sheerline, 21–**22**
righting moment, 63–64, **65**, **66**
rigid inflatable boats (RIBs), **139–42**
round-bilge hulls, 3, **27**–31
    bow shape, 28–**29**
    buttock lines, **18**
    flare, 29
    freeboard, 30–31
    keel, 31
    lines plan drawing, **16–17**
    midbody, 29, **30**
    sea comfort of, 28
    skegs, 31
    stability, **62**
    stern, 29–30
round-chine hull, **19**
rowing shells, 34
rudders, 121–22
rudderstock, **116**
running strakes, 23, **24**. *See also* strakes

S
Sabreline 43, **43**
safety
    deck design and, 75–76, 77
    hull construction, 138
    lighting, 77–78
    sheerline and, **52**
saltwater flats boats, 40–**41**
seat design, **77**, **79**–80
seaworthiness, 3–4, 6–9
    cabin design, 69–70
    deck design, 70–71
    engine room, 70
    freeboard and, 6–7
    hull shapes and, 69
    skipper judgment and, 68–69
seaworthiness factors by hull shape, 8–9
sectional view of lines plan, 18–19
    lobster-boat-style hull, **16–17**
    V-hull boats, **14–15**, **33**
Seemann Composite Resin Infusion Molding
    (SCRIMP), 128, 130, 132
semicustom boat construction, 138
semidisplacement hulls. *See* semiplaning hulls
semiplaning hulls, 31, 43–44
    bow shape, 44
    compared to planing, 44
    flare, 23
    midbody, 44–45
    skeg, 45
    speed and, 4–6
    stern, 45

S-glass, **126**, 127, 133
shaft logs, 97, 104
sheerline, **51**
    deep-V hull, **39**
    development in wooden boats, 51
    discontinuous, 52
    false, 52
    reverse, 21–**22**, 36–**37**
    styling, 50–**52**, **53**
side thrust
    fuel efficiency and, 108
    handling and, 109
skegs
    round-bilge hull, 31
    semidisplacement hulls, 45
    V-hull boats, 34
ski boats, **38**
skipper judgment, and seaworthiness, 68–69
slim hulls, 34. *See also* catamarans
    heel angle in, 34
    lack of accommodations, 34
    stability, 34
Smullins, Joe, 114
soft-chine hull, **19**
speed, 46
    comfort and, 10–11, 72–73
    displacement–length ratio, 47
    limiting factors, 4–6
    propeller adjustment and, 109
    stern shape and, **18**
    trade-off with range and comfort, 3
speed–length ratio (S/L), 47
speed-power curve, 4–6, **5**
sportfishing boats, 44, **62**
    flare, 23
squat, 5–6, **18**
stability, about
    calculating, 65
    center of gravity and, 63–64
    chines, 64
    cockpit flooding and, 66–**67**
    deadrise and, 20–**21**
    engine placement and, 33
    hull shapes and, **61–62**
    length-to-beam ratio, 48, 61
    measurement of, 60
    restoring moment, **65**
    righting moment, 63–64, **65**, **66**
    slim hulls, 34
    tender and stiff boats, 64
    V-hull boats, 33–34, 75
stability, types of
    form, 60–**62**
    longitudinal, 60, 64, 65
    transverse, 60, 65

weight, 60
stabilizers
    active, **74**–75
    antiroll tanks, 73–**74**
    flopper stoppers, 75
    flume tanks, 73–**74**
    paravanes, 75
    passive, 73–**74**
stacks, 58
stairwells, 76–77
standing headroom, **80**
stateroom, 73
steering systems, about, 115
    maintenance, 83
steering systems, types of
    electric, **121**
    rack-and-pinion, 120–21
    rudders, 121–22
    tiller, 120
    wheel, 115–**19**, **121**
    whipstaff, 119–**20**
steering with twin engines, 122
stepped hulls, **39**
sterndrive engines, **101–2**
stern seal, 97
stern shape, 55
    deep-V hulls, 39
    for outboard engines, 91–92
    planing hulls, 36
    round-bilge hulls, 29–30
    semidisplacement hull, 45
    speed and, **18**
    V-hull boats, 34
stern squat, 5–6, **18**
stern tube, 97
stiff boats, 63, 64
storage
    anchor, 85–86
    cabin sole, under, 85
    electronics, 84
    engine room, 85
    galley, 84
    lockers, 84
    overhead, 85
    refrigerator, 84–85
strakes
    deep-V hulls, 37
    hull design feature, 23, **24**
    lifting in deep-V hull, **39**
    lifting in planing hulls, 36
    placement in deep-V hulls, **38**
    V-hull boats, **14–15**
Stratos 21XL Magnum bass boat, **41**
strongback, 123
stuffing box, 97, 104

superstructure styling, **55**–57
Suzuki EFI engine, 94–**95**

T
Teleflex MPS hydraulic steering system, **117**
tender boats, 63, 64
tiller steering systems, 120
torque, 100, 108–9
tow, 126–27
Transcat 48, **35**
transitional hulls. *See* semiplaning hulls
transmission, 97, 103–4
transom design. *See* stern shape
transom-stern sportfishing boats, stability, **62**
transverse stability, 60, 65
trawler style yacht, 26–27
triaxial fabric, 127
trim angle, **24–25**
trimarans, 34
trim flaps, to increase wake, 38
trim tabs, **24–25**, 41
trolling motors, electric, **100**–101
tug yacht, **137**
turbine engine, **2**
Turbinia, 34
turbocharger, in diesel engine, 98, 99
twin engines
    compared to single, 99–101
    cost considerations, 100–101
    steering with, 122
two-stroke cycle engines, 88–**89**
    Mercury Optimax, 95, **96**
    Suzuki EFI, 94–**95**
    Yamaha HPDI, 92, 93–**94**

U
U.S. Coast Guard rescue boat, 6, **7**
U.S. Environmental Protection Agency (EPA),
    92

V
vacuum-assisted resin transfer molding
        (VARTM), 128, 130–32, **131**
vacuum bagging, 128, 129
vertical center of buoyancy (VCB), 60–**62**
vertical center of gravity (VCG), 60–**62**, 65
V-hull boats, 31–34. *See also* deep-V hulls
    bow shape, 31–**32**
    cabin design, 33
    chines, **19**, 31–**33**, 33
    coastal cruising boat, **11**
    deadrise, 31

V-hull boats *(continued)*
    flare, 31
    lines plan drawing, **14–15**
    power cruiser, **32**
    sectional view, **33**
    skeg, 34
    stability and, 33–34
    stern, 34
vibration, in engines, 111–12
vinylester resin, 135
Virtual Engineered Composites (VEC), **132**
volatile organic compounds (VOC), 129, 130

W
wakeboarding boats, **6**, 38
walk the stern, 100
walkways, 81
waterskiing boats, **38**
Wave Piercer, 2–**3**
weight stability, 60
Wellcraft 35 Scarab Sport, **42**

Wellcraft 350 Coastal, **11**
Wellcraft 270 Coastal Fisherman, **40**, **58**
Wellcraft Excalibur SCS, **22**
Wellcraft 8300 Martinique, **11**
WEST System, 137
wheel steering systems, types of, 115–**16**
    cable, 118
    hydraulic, **116–17**, **121**
    wire, 118–**19**
whipstaff steering systems, 119–**20**
wire steering systems, 118–**19**
wooden boats sheerline, 51

Y
Yamaha HPDI engine, 92, 93–**94**
Yamaha VMax 250 hp engine, **41**
Yanmar 6C-ETE 420 hp diesel engine, **98**

Z
Zodiac RIB, **139**